Flow Freedom Laws of the World™

FLOW Freedom Laws of the World™

"Catch the Wave" to your Current of Creativity

DR. CHRISTOPHER TEMPORELLI

Blue Wizard Press

Thoughts on the FLOW Freedom Laws of the World ™

Linda Arsenio, actress, model, star of Hindi film hits such as *Kabul Express*...

"*Christopher Temporelli takes readers on an inspiring, magical, and exciting journey in this beautifully laid out and practical step-by-step guidebook to catapulting one's life to the next level. A must-read for anyone seeking direction or simply wanting to love and appreciate their life as it is—right now. Temporelli's FLOW System has truly motivated me to take immediate action in my own life with great enthusiasm and utter positivity. A priceless gem for these trying times that one can anchor onto for a lifetime. Read this book—and be ready for authentic joy & success!*"

Linda Jeon and **Mansik Jeong**, Film and TV actors, theater impresarios, reality TV star, celebrity couple, films including...*Asura, the Tiger, Money*...

"*We admire Christopher Temporelli's creative output, he is a compelling artist as well as a brilliant business entrepreneur, and we are excited for his book's publication...it is a way to bring people closer together as they follow their individual paths. And we find it so beautiful to watch the author follow his calling in this country, we call Korea.*"

Mike Figgis, filmmaker, musician, Academy Award nominated director for the film, *Leaving Las Vegas*...

"I'm reading Christopher Temporelli's FLOW in a quarantine approved hotel in Hong Kong. With two weeks of isolation ahead of me, I contemplate my place in the universal map. The book taps into many of the issues we are all experiencing right now and the author shares with us his travel experiences and insights with disarming charm."

Hyun Jun Jang, producer *BEFM English Radio* and former Lieutenant, Korean Special Forces.

"This is a story full of energy...and if anyone met Christopher in person, or heard his radio program, one might have already felt his energy even before starting the book...this story helps us find our way in life."

Myung Chan Kang, film producer, hit films including: *Ashfall, Take point, C'est si bon*...

"FLOW Freedom Laws of the World™ is designed to provide opportunities to discover those fountains of wisdom inside us. I believe the sparkling insights in this book will light your way like a lighthouse standing out against the dark sky."

Barbara Pyle, filmmaker, executive producer and co-creator of the TV series *Captain Planet and the Planeteers* and major supporter of the *Planeteer Movement*.

"As I live on a remote island, I have just received and begun my copy of the FLOW Freedom Laws of the World ™. However, knowing Christopher as I do, I can state with certainty that the book will be complex and multi-faceted, yet fun, engaging, insightful, empathetic and compassionate—and most likely off-the-charts brilliant. Christopher is a star among stars. I am honored that he thinks of himself as a Planeteer and is a founding member of the Global Planeteer Movement."

Louis Tallarini, Real estate and banking investor, former Chairman of the Board of Governors of the *Singers Forum Foundation*, the *Columbus Citizens Foundation* and currently the Chairman of the *Italian Language Foundation*.

"Go with the FLOW, Chris!!!! Knowing you as a professional and as a friend over these many years, it makes me proud to understand how grounded you are...now I know why. This advance copy of your book FLOW Freedom Laws of the World ™ reminds me of the relaxation meditation classes at the Singers Forum where we first encountered each other. FLOW is a great read and will help all who indulge reach their inner self and FLOW..."

Contents

Thoughts On The FLOW Freedom Laws Of The World ™   iv
Copyright   x
Dedication   xi
Foreword   xiii

Title Page   1

Images   3

FLOW Freedom Laws Of The World ™   5

Prescript   7

PART I   11

Prologue   13

City of temples   16

The need for FLOW   27

Introduction FLOW Freedom Laws of the World ™   31

Potential   35

Choices	38

PART II 43

FLOW Freedom Laws Of The World ™ 45

FLOW Law 1	47
FLOW Law 2	62
FLOW Law 3	80
FLOW Law 4	102
FLOW Law 5	123
FLOW Law 6	138
FLOW Law 7	151

PART III 165

Conclusion	167
Arrange your direction and FLOW	168
Let your life FLOW around new goals	170
Family and friends	171
Get the skills as easily as you can	173

Your FLOW team and the idea of mentorship	176
Keep following the dream	178
Watch and enjoy the FLOW	180
Unlocking an 8th Law	184
Endnotes	186
Author	187

FLOW Freedom Laws of the World™*
"Catch the Wave" to your Current of Creativity
Copyright © 2021 Dr. Christopher Temporelli
All rights reserved. This book or any portion thereof may not be reproduced or used in any manner whatsoever without the express written permission of the author or publisher.

*(FLOW Freedom Laws of the World™ at time of publication is under registration review by the United States Patent and Trademark Office.)

Pine Wizard Press

Book jacket author photo, credit: Won Seok Chang.
Manuscript critique: credit to Ashley Henshaw
and *The Artful Editor.*
Special thanks: Percy Dorian Lee for considerations of style.

Disclaimers: This book is an exploration of practical philosophy and is not meant to diagnosis or treat any condition or serve as financial counsel. Neither the publisher nor author guarantee results, and it is understood examples given in the text are often extraordinary. Results may vary.

Certain specific names in the text deemed auxiliary have been omitted or obscured, and although the publisher and the author have made every effort to ensure that the information in this book was correct at press time, the publisher and the author assume no responsibility for errors, inaccuracies, omissions, or any other inconsistencies herein and hereby disclaim any liability.

Hard cover First Printing, 2021

With many thanks to everyone who helped make this book possible—and the FLOW itself. Special thanks to Dr. Baskaran Pillai, who in the courtyard of a former Brahmin residence surrounded by the rich cultural artifacts of India, under the light of a Vedic moon, recommended I take a journey...

Foreword

Alicia Olatuja

The Beauty of FLOW

This beautifully written and incredibly insightful book not only gifts the reader with the understanding of how to surrender to the current of life and self-actualization, but it also provides a roadmap to look back over your life and see where the beauty of FLOW was present and active in possibly some of the most monumental and even the seemingly coincidental moments of life!

I remember when I stood on the steps of the U.S. Capital and sang as soloist for the second Inauguration of President Barack Obama, I kept wondering how this opportunity had come into my life and what would be the next steps in my journey as a vocal artist.

FLOW Freedom Laws of the World ™ provides the blueprint to being able to trust the process of living life with an openness to embrace the road ahead—while basking in the essence of moment-to-moment existence.

Alicia Olatuja
Recording Artist, Voice Instructor,
Founder / Creator of Vocal Breakthrough Academy.

Title page

FLOW

Freedom

Laws

of the

World ™

"Catch the Wave" to your

Current of Creativity

Dr. Christopher Temporelli, DMA

Images

(photos credit to author, unless notated)

Temple gate in Tamil Nadu, India...15
Crystal form of Lord Ganesh with mountain view...24
Sunset over the Bay of Bengal, India...27
Chalong Temple, Phuket, Thailand...37
Waves on Marina Beach, Chennai, India...49
Author taking a moment in Shanghai, China...58
Traditional park, Beijing, China...67
Share D Table restaurant, Seoul, South Korea...74
A path or "Way" leading around Shuri Castle, ...77
Naha city, Okinawa, Japan
Example of FLOW Law 3, 3-step process...82
Promo photo of the author (credit: Estro Studio)...86
View of Manhattan from Sunset Park, Brooklyn...96
Angor Wat, Cambodia...108
Temple in the tundra, Inner Mongolia, China...114
The author on boat, Lake Atitlan, Guatemala...116
Sky above La Grande-Motte, French Alps...121
Dong Baek Island, Busan, South Korea...125
Author photo, Waldorf Astoria New York, Gala...142
Promo-photo for author as co-owner / sommelier: ...156
Share D Table restaurant, Seoul, South Korea
Belizean coastline...177
Chosŏn-era pagoda, (eight-sided tower) ...183
Seoul, South Korea

FLOW Freedom Laws of the World ™

FLOW Law 1 - "Catch the Wave"

FLOW Law 2 - "Love the Wave"

FLOW Law 3 - "List the Wave"

FLOW Law 4 - "Time the Wave"

FLOW Law 5 - "Zen the Wave"

FLOW Law 6 - "Honor the Waves"

FLOW Law 7 - "Surf the Wave"

Prescript

Messages from the subconscious, or superconscious, the ether, or the Akash—however you'd like to call it—can arrive as a pre-set package. It was said, Mozart dictated by pen music which arrived already assembled in his mind. This book hit me in the like.

While musing on a comprehensive theory, a "how to" for existence, this book's form in one swoop dropped to my mind as if from heaven. Admittedly, a culmination of an intellectual and experiential process developed over a lifetime, however, when it "dropped," it was in a codified form. It appeared in this guise of the FLOW Freedom Laws of the World ™. In other words, it felt inspired.

This book can guide you to peace of mind, and along with that, it can serve as your handbook or map to success. Perhaps most importantly, in the success in enjoying success—which are not necessarily correlated. The desire for development is limitless—and this book assists reaching life ambitions; personal ambitions, career or wealth ambitions, ambitions for family or relationships—and along with it, why not enjoy the process?

This work is a magnum opus for those seeking this type of knowledge, for a framework to organize personal experience, and it can be approached in several ways. It is a good story—even exciting at times. It traverses the globe, from the temples of Tamil Nadu, India to the FLOW's hit outside a mega shopping mall in Busan, South Korea. It gives an insider's glance to a trendy market style restaurant in Seoul, South Korea, treks to the jungles of Cambodia and Central America, and reminisces on concert appearances across Caribbean Islands and North America, including in Ottawa, Canada and in New York City...along with detailing the occasional celebrity encounter.

Stories are woven around a set of principles, most notably, these FLOW Freedom Laws of the World ™ (FLOW System) which are shown as guidelines or foundations of a creative process. This achievement of one's creative state is investigated as the true foundation of success. Capsulizing this theory, the guidelines and processes simultaneously form a philosophy of life—for well-being, contentment, and peace of mind—as well as the method to "up" potential to reach whatever it is you desire.

Having a profound philosophy available is always useful, and especially valid in times of personal and even global upheaval. If you are starting out in life and wish for more direction, or find yourself in a position where tides are changing and you need direction or focus for what is to come—investigate this theory. And if you find yourself in a state of general apprehension for the world at large, even perhaps your place in it, read on!

The book is a message of hope and...fun. And again, if you have ambition, if you hope to ramp up for extraordinary experiences and level-up to peak performance—where you may change not only yourself, but even the world—this is a method for you.

If you resonate with this reference, for this type of wisdom even, the framework you find here is exceptional and life changing. *Part I* gives background and the FLOW Laws in action on an extraordinary tour in India. *Part II* contains the "how to" section, where the FLOW Freedom Laws of the World ™ themselves are revealed and discussed. Then final thoughts and the conclusion take place in *Part III.*

This book is not merely theoretical in nature, but practical. It portrays a method tested, based not only on deep study and philosophy, but also picturesque and easily applied. Already this method is serving many adherents well, it has universal appeal—though how you employ it is completely individual, it's up to you...

Best wishes and follow your FLOW!

Dr. Christopher Temporelli, DMA
Busan, Republic of Korea, Sept. 15, 2020

PART I

Prologue

A late spring in the air, I was at ease and content. My plane landed at Chennai International Airport on a local flight departing from central Tamil Nadu, India. Finding an eager and friendly local taxi driver outside the arrival terminal, we set off to my hotel for the evening.

The hotel, in my estimation, is one of the most elegant, tasteful—one of the most luxurious in India. Located a distance from the airport on a special position overlooking the sea, it affords splendid views of the Indian Ocean.

I asked the driver how long until we reached the hotel. He said 30 minutes...or one hour...dependent on the traffic. We pulled out of the airport into the traffic, I called from the back seat, "One hour!" He really laughed, "Oh, that's a good one, sir."

I reclined and drank in the drive. The multi-colored whirling and swirling of Chennai life as viewed through the taxi window entranced me. My body sank into the seat from the combination of effort and accomplishment that had been the day. I had finished a monumental, pre-determined visit to ancient monuments and temples.

The sites were inland in southern India, approximately a one-hour flight from Chennai, India. It had been an exceptional day, and the drive returning from this adventure was one to savor.

Traveling the globe has become a lifestyle, and along with the thrill of a great vacation, travel adventure is a chance for change. This journey we are about to investigate was a chance to reset my life. It was a rare experience.

Connecting with your FLOW, you might find yourself drawn to new experiences, possibly on numerous levels. This can even simply be a shift in perspective. Of course, a trip or pilgrimage is a method of change and growth long honored in the history of humanity. Today, you might call it "vacation." By moving location, even a relatively short distance, you can potentially change your direction in life.

To punctuate my life, or work out new directions, or just for the thrill of it, I have taken numerous...well, vacations with pilgrimage intent. This one to Tamil Nadu was about the purist "pilgrimage" of them all. Regarding the idea of a pilgrimage to India, interesting to note, when Mark Zuckerberg craved inspiration, he traversed his own temple trip in India, on recommendation of Steve Jobs. One could infer there is something to this concept.

Temple gate in Tamil Nadu, India

City of temples

Prior to this airport arrival in Chennai, planning, intention, and advising sought for this outing far outpaced that of a relaxing vacation. My life had been transiting, after counsel with a prominent mentor, a course of action was initiated. I sought further specific guidance for this "spirit quest" and an itinerary of pilgrimage to six temples emerged.

These temples located in central Tamil Nadu, exist in a temple vortex centered around Kumbakonam, a town encompassing a nexus of temples in South India. Known as "city of temples," Kumbakonam is considered a key to alter one's life-course. A powerful thought. I had lit-up with intention for growth and development and finding a focal point for this ambition as a journey pleased me.

In many traditional cultures, finding a focus or quest for change is embedded in the mass consciousness. Some Indian or Vedic traditions view this process, and specifically this area in India, as a vehicle to clear or resolve personal emanations—even from one's past lives. My mind was intrigued with possibilities of results from such an adventure.

Temples on my itinerary were partially located in populated areas, yet some were nestled in rural and remote South India. Temples stood ancient, and with this antiquity came an aura of the mysterious and sacred. Indeed, a unique pilgrimage.

I have traveled the globe, with many locations I cherish, yet Tamil Nadu holds a special place in my heart. The temples are remarkable. To tread those paths is a walk into a wholly other place and time. Transformative.

For this specific trip, the timing was extraordinary. Arising partly from attention to planning, but mostly I simply showed up at the right time at the right place. It was lucky. The local Tamil people called it a blessing of the gods.

I followed basic realities (temple opening times) along with guidelines and principles adhering to local thought or older systems of knowledge, such as Vedic thought and astrology. This included visiting temples on days or hours considered auspicious to the presiding deity. I did my utmost to understand this world and honor its tradition.

One example of auspicious timing appeared at a Muruga Temple, around Swamimalai, on the outskirts of the city of Kumbakonam. Muruga is a deity, a son of the great god Shiva, and this deity, Muruga, historically is profoundly revered by the Tamil people. This particular temple in Swamimalai is considered a significant sacred space.

Arriving at the central shrine of this temple, a ceremony commenced. This was an auspicious sign, to witness the rite performed. Maneuvering the throng, I twisted and wedged myself a space on the stone floor in a central zone with full view of the priests and shrine. I observed the libation of the statuesque form of the deity as water, ghee (clarified butter) and liquids imbued with what appeared golden turmeric, poured over his form. The statue, clothed in fine raiment, after a veiling process, was then revealed to devotees and worshipers with candles, chimes, and exclamations.

Another visit, early morning of that flight day back to Chennai, the timing was even more extraordinary. Making our way to the temple, my guide purchased entry tickets and I advanced to the main sanctuary. Precisely as I stepped into the central sanctum, bells and horns announced the coming of priests and a parade of temple luminaries appeared.

This day I was first in line for the central temple! I had stepped foot into the sanctuary at the precise moment.

After an initial blessing from the priest arriving with his entourage, I descended a stair deep into one of the stone-walled inner chambers of the temple. It was hot down there, incense burned and candles illuminated, but there was no other source of light. With little movement of air, the place was thick with the incense and the smell of flame and time.

A new priest appeared, he was ancient, wizened—in need of a little modern dentistry—but spectacular and all details added to the moment. I found myself yearning for the blessing of this priest, and of this temple. I sensed the transient nature of time and knew there existed one chance for this encounter. This temple embodied a special archetype of power and knowledge, and I wished to meet the opportunity ready.

Along with all other features, this temple houses a sacred spring that flows to it from deep in the Earth. It is said to feed spiritual power and significance to the place. I felt this idea—and more—present in this hidden subterranean chamber and this moment in time.

Emotion touched me and I turned to the priest. We looked at each other straight in the eyes, this priest and I, and I empathized his recognition of my intent and sincerity. Singular human experience transcended; my mind opened to vast connectedness. We paused in that moment and then in Tamil or ancient Sanskrit, he gave an invocation and raised his hand in a sign of blessing.

Coming to the final temple, just before the flight back to Chennai, you can imagine, I was prepared to repeat this magical timing. Ready for the warm acceptance and immediacy of the other temple visits. Temple tickets in hand, we approached the entrance to the main sanctuary.

There was a sign that stated, "Hindus only" which I barely bothered to notice. If not strictly "Hindu," I looked and felt authentic, like I belonged there, a pilgrim, a seeker—a devotee. Whatever I was supposed to look like, I looked like it. Or so I thought.

As I attempted the entry to the inner temple, the guard gave me a once over and made a "no-go" gesture. I took it in stride, I had been welcomed at all other temples. I sagely understood he would quickly realize his error in judgement. Snaping to my senses, it was soon apparent I was being comprehended as "touristic," and would not be allowed admittance.

My guide calmly explained this American was sincere and serious. I was in appropriate temple clothes, had the sacred, holy ash (vibhuti) and red kumkum (special vermilion powder) on my forehead from the previous temple. I had the appropriate offering for the deity, flowers and herbs, all arranged in bags from the vendors at the temple gate. I was prepared.

The temple guard gave me another look and then a stern gesture, "No, no." My guide heated up, gesturing, and explaining other temples—and even the various gods—had accepted me. I offered a tentative smile and little wave of hello.

Without speaking any English or Tamil, the answer from the guard was clear, "No way...not on my watch." My guide was not holding his calm as well as he had. In my mind's eye, I saw an image of heated debate from a local herb market—one could imagine where this was heading. It was time to disengage. As I edged away, I turned to my guide and asked, "What next?!"

This was our final stop on the tour. After our time together, he realized my seriousness to complete the journey. But all considered, including the schedule for an upcoming flight, he devised a plan to drop the offering at the shrine across the portico and make a quick exit.

I did not see this plan emerge, until my guide took my offering toward the other shrine's priests. I can understand his mind. We had already completed a full time together and he was ready to wrap things up.

This shrine across from the main sanctuary was honoring the god Garuda. Garuda is a legendary bird-like divinity, also said to be a vehicle of the god Vishnu. The priests were beautiful and fine appearing people. Their eyes and minds struck me as clear and sharp…possibly birdlike…they would not accept an offering intended for the main sanctuary. I agreed as well, it was not the purpose for which we came.

I wished a "good vibe" with these wardens of the shrine, I was indeed in one of India's sacred spaces. And I also wished for the good grace of the divinity, Garuda. I put my hand over my heart in Tamil fashion and made a small bow to the priests. I thanked them, naturally including the so-called "Indian head nod" (where one's head sort of pivots left and right) and felt relaxation in the atmosphere. Apology accepted. I backed away and brought my guide along with me. What next? …now my guide was ready for action! To the office of the temple manager!

We hurried to his office. The manager heard the story. He smiled. He nodded. He agreed. He understood everything, and what luck, he was happy to help! But, of course, after lunch. At this time, the temple entrance was now closed.

"What time did the entrance close?" I asked. "A quarter past the hour," came the answer. At that moment, the clock hand clicked to 16 minutes past the hour. We left the office, and ok, I was ready for the next step, "What now?" My guide shrugged, "To the airport." I respond with, "Ok, we check in and then can come back, right? There is time for that before the flight?"

I could not imagine missing the culmination of this trip. He smiled at my naïveté, he smiled a mix of dejection and good humor at my eagerness and conviction. He attempted to console...we did our best, so many good temples... This is just one and we had a good run. Sometimes that is just the way it is.

An impulse like a bolt of lightning ran through me. The FLOW hit. I circumvented the globe to Tamil Nadu to complete these six temples. This was a mission of spirit. This was meant to be completed and I was not to be held back by a well-intended—but misguided! —temple guard.

For a split second, I said nothing to my guide. Then quickly grabbed the offering he was holding...and I ran. I literally *ran* back to the temple. I yelled over my shoulder, "I will be back!"

I knew there was no time left, it must now be at 18 minutes past the hour. I remember my white cotton pants swishing back and forth and the temple was huge...will I make the right turns?... Upon entering the temple, I maintained enough self-awareness to mask the appearance of my movement to a fast walk as I made my way to the main sanctuary.

Approaching the entrance to the main sanctuary, the guard concurrently allowed two women into the gate—who were also running in as dignified a fashion as possible, colorful saris (Indian flowing garments) billowing out around them. It must have been getting on five minutes after the official closing time, however, the women's entrance gave me courage. I marched directly up to the guard. He looked at me as if to say, "What are *you* doing back here."

And then I simultaneously surprised the guard, and myself. I spontaneously lifted my hand in a gesture of benediction and in a classically trained bass voice invoked a mantra or invocation of Lord Ganesh. A great mantra. A chant to the first god worshipped in ceremonies and the deity known as the Destroyer of Obstacles.

"OM, GUM GANAPATAYE, NAMAHA!"

He looked at me utterly dumbfounded. Stunned. My inner thought process marveled, "Wow, did I just do that." Yet, I looked at him directly in the eyes, I even squinted just a little...let him know I meant business... Again, full, direct, confident, and quite fast...

"OM, GUM GANAPATAYE, NAMAHA!"

In a traditional mind this *must* be directly inspired by the god! I finished the final sound "HA" with a very definitive, very convincingly intoned, and authoritative sound. And then we both paused. Everything went silent. We just looked at each other. We did not move. We did not breath. After a few moments, my senses started to return and the thought, "Oh, wow, did I really just do that?!" passed through my mind. I glanced back at him for an answer.

He rocked his head contemplatively back and forth a few times. Raised an eyebrow. Paused. Then gave me a quick nod of his head towards the inner sanctum. Excitement rushed through me, but I could not yet believe it.

I raised both eyebrows, nodded my own head back and forth rapidly, and then made a quick gesture with head and hand towards the entrance (really, in there?!) —along with a quizzical and probably slightly comical look.

He exhaled and rocked his head back and forth. Stopped. Held still. And then the look, "Better go now before I change my mind." I did not hesitate; I was already into the temple—I had come a *long* way.

Speeding into the temple, the whole mantra experience was spinning in my mind. It stunned me as much as it stunned the guard. That is one of the points of being in the FLOW. When your commitment to a process arrives at a certain level, and you find yourself in a creative state where the things you wish simply *must* happen, that is one example of what I call being in the FLOW. And when you are in the FLOW (that is a culmination of employing the FLOW Freedom Laws of the World ™) things seem to happen. Spontaneity happens. It is a phenomenon.

I followed the way deeper into the sanctum. Depending on ticket type, there were various railing lined paths leading into the inner temple. More expensive tickets were meant for expediated entry, and of course, my ticket was somewhere outside the temple with my guide...

This is an important point that can arise. Sometimes jumping into your FLOW, you might recognize, you have no idea how you got where you are...and then what to do next! Which way to go?! At that moment, I had left my guide on the doorstop. Sometimes as we jump fully into the current of existence, it can be fun, but also a little unnerving. It is times like these when we need to check back into ourselves and find the way anew.

A thought—or a request—flooded my mind with an image of the god Ganesh. Ultimately, my thoughts circled, it was His mantra appearing like a *deus ex machina*[1] which had cleared my path. I felt, in a mystical way, the mantra appeared to secure my entrance. I brought the image of Ganesh to my mind, and had a thought or prayer pass through, as I beseeched continued guidance.

As I was hesitating, looking right and left, at an impasse as where to next, a yet more inner temple guard spotted me. Surprised to see me there, he called me to him through a certain gate. I arrived a little breathless, stopped just in front of him and we regarded each other for a moment. Silence. I gave him another sheepish smile and took one more moment to reorganize myself. He looked at me as if I were the strangest thing he had ever seen. "Where is your ticket...are you *even* Hindu?"

Crystal form of Lord Ganesh with mountain view

"Oh, sorry, well, sort of...the ticket's outside...uh, I've got cash?!" Awkward pause, and...

"OM, GUM GANAPATAYE, NAMAHA!'"

I did it again. He froze. No response. Then after a few seconds in a soft, beautiful south Indian accent. "Can you do that again?" I invoked the chant yet again. He became the next in a line of stunned guards. He called over his counterpart. "Hey, come listen to this guy. UH, can you do that again??..." Why not...

"OM, GUM GANAPATAYE, NAMAHA"

They froze in a comic-book-style silence. As the guard came back to himself, he declared, ... "GO!"

"I don't have a ticket!" I declared. "Just GO!" He stated, and began waving his arms around in no direction in particular. I took off. I made it around a corner. Another man with a ticket basket looking stern...*Here we go again.*

He commenced articulations in Tamil with the English word "ticket" inserted into the rampage. Turning the corner behind me the previous guard appeared. He retorted back in Tamil at the basket holder, then exclaimed to me, "Go, GO!"

Working my way through a final bit of this labyrinth, it was time to brush down and arrange my garments, slow the pace, and enter the inner sanctum. Gratitude welled up in my eyes. "How could I have made it this far?!"

What a satisfyingly fantastic feeling! Now, life does not always have to be that intense...I don't want that much intensity every day! But this was a special trip and the accomplishment washed over me, I made it. And this meant more to me than just having physically entered a temple in that moment, I had also made it to my FLOW.

The last few devotees in line from the morning regarded me with curiosity, but kindly. It became my turn to stand in front of the priests at the main altar. They smiled at me, took me aside and accepted my offering. Explaining the significance of the temple, they blessed my forehead with more holy ash and gave me a lotus.

I felt contentment. Very, very content. And grateful.

The need for FLOW

Sunset over the Bay of Bengal, India

This experience in the temple gives a taste of being in your FLOW. It is to be perceptive (even to subtleties), to be re-active, to aim for your goals and concurrently follow developments as they emerge. It is getting the job done, even if all chance seems finished, and the easiest thing to do is to give-up and head to the airport. It is that mix of self-engineering and trust, a creative spirit of inspiration that seems to come from beyond ourselves. This could be the finish to an introduction...but the waves from this experience kept rippling along.

After this final temple visit's completion, my guide and I leisurely made our way to the airport. We lunched and then I was in the air for the hour's flight. And with that, this story returns to where this "Prologue" began, in a taxi to a hotel in Chennai, overlooking the sea.

I arrived at the hotel that evening, at ease, and confident. I settled in and unpacked, I luxuriated in the hotel surroundings, it was a transformation from my picturesque, but more rustic lodgings in central Tamil Nadu. I viewed the ocean from the hotel room. Then I arranged myself on a couch beside a lithe and mysterious statue of a deity in the hotel rear lobby and gazed again on the sea. Then I descended steps to a portico behind the hotel for some last moments of light glimmering over the water. You get the idea, I was at peace, in a kind of bliss.

At the evening dinner, I chose the main dining hall and an animated, good natured waiter appeared to illuminate the menu. He was in his early twenties, charming and we joked about this and that and worked through the menu together.

To give a sense of the evening, it was a fine hotel, and I fully attired myself for dinner. I maintained the vibhuti and kumkum on my forehead (marks of holy ash and special vermilion powder) from the temples and I was draped in my most lavish and expensive set of Indian traditional clothing I had acquired. And, more than my regalia, I radiated peace and contentment. I just did. I could feel it. Everyone seemed to feel it.

The waiter unsuccessfully attempted to cloak his curiosity. Curiosity with my attire, my state of mind, and my Tamil Nadu temple tour. Though native to India, he had visited temples or significant sites only on rare occasions. He explained to me, he and his friends had made their way to temples merely a few times, sensing a power or antiquity in their experience, but rarely had he ever stepped foot on one of these sites. Thus, I was for him a being—foreign, curious, and outlandish.

Without prompting after the wine arrived, I with my attention on the arrival of a nice Merlot, he stepped back from the table. The dial of the mood intensified, as he mentioned something of a family issue—around his incessant motor scooter racing, I think—and then a surprise.

After these temple visits, all of this curious, introspective and spiritual inquiry—and my looking much too much at peace—he asked, "Please, give me the meaning of life!"

"This must be a jest," I thought. I looked back from my Merlot—it was a fine choice by the way—however, I detected no levity in his features. Utterly serious. Now I felt curiosity and surprise. His eyes, momentarily strained and tightened, peered at me—and at my fine Merlot—in sincerity.

My perception of hotel surroundings, restaurant, even the Merlot, vanished. There we were, two human beings, together, alone with only the existential questions. My amusing waiter disappearing, now I accompanied a young person grasping for peace of mind. Perhaps recent family friction opened an existential angst... My heart was moved, commitment arose, and I decided to give a best attempt to his question.

It is interesting in times of great emotional, psychological, or spiritual stress, many will face their existential questions. And this is also the time probably least fitting to deal with the big questions. The loss of a job, even if relatively easily remedied, can open a whole host of questions regarding meaning and purpose. This can be ultimately useful but might be more comfortably addressed in a stable state. But then again, stability might not provide the incentive or pressure to introspect.

I began the process of addressing my young questioner, pointing out his question for the meaning of life was quite a "large order." The pun was intended and served the purpose to lighten the mood. "And by the way," I stated, "Who promised you there would be just one meaning…"

Then I commenced in earnest to satisfy his question, resolve his dilemma, and bring him some peace. I explained the basics of what is FLOW Law 1. I asked, could we switch from "What is the meaning of life," to "How can we most skillfully navigate this world that we encounter." "Can we think less about the ultimate meaning of life, allow Life—for the time being at least—to take care of itself? And in its stead, we can engulf ourselves in our direct moment of existence," as in FLOW Law 1: "Catch the Wave."

Instead of, "Why?" we court existence's friendship, ascending to the crest of life in this here and now, this time and place, and *thereby* solidifying our meaning. The "meaning of life," then, requires no answer, outside of a connection to Life itself.

There was silence as I finished speaking, and he registered the experience. He was stunned. Flabbergasted might be a more descriptive word. He had surprised himself when he asked for the meaning of life, and that I actually answered him, even more. These few moments left a visceral impact.

He was brighter and the mood again lightened. I felt tremendous fulfillment to see another human, even for a short time, at ease and happy. Later, as he and another staff walked me back to the hotel after dessert, he was thankful for the insight. Though so simple a shift, the impact could be meteoric.

Walking a flower strewn corridor back into the central hotel, wide windows afforded a view over the hotel entry's reflecting pool. At this time in the evening, flame *fountains* had been ignited, and danced around, reflecting off the pool. Contemplatively, as I made my way, our humanity's continued need for answers struck me.

Introduction FLOW Freedom Laws of the World ™

The premise for this book came on the spot—at once. It landed in my mind, out of the blue, a few weeks after returning from India while strolling at a shopping mall in South Korea. At the time, I had just finished a late lunch at the mall after having stopped by the radio station (where I host a music program) earlier that day.

I was taking my time, enjoying the high-end shops pass by as I worked my way to exit the mall and return home. I had been musing some on my recent experiences, but I was not—in those exact moments—actively seeking a revelation. Creativity, however, or the FLOW, often has a timing of its own. It was as I moved through the front doors of the structure to exit the building when this revelation appeared.

And this revelation was the clear structuring of the FLOW Law system, and its appearance was extraordinary! My travel journey emerged as inspiration to illuminate, frame, and simultaneously serve as template, demonstrating the FLOW Freedom Laws of the World ™ in action. The emergence at that instant was another illumination, that plan as one may, answers sometimes arrive once we relax, or are at ease enough, for the process to deeply integrate and appear in its own time.

Writing the book itself continued as an example of the FLOW Laws in action. The creative principle had appeared, then I needed to catch onto this wave of the book. We will discuss details in a later section, but after the excitement of the initial idea that first day, it was necessary to keep this wave flowing the next day when there was an opportunity to start writing.

And that next day commenced the process of upping the positivity, motivation, and momentum, following the principles, fleshing out the details, and keeping with it. This book's history in and of itself is an example of creation showing itself within creation.

Though the set appearance of the FLOW Laws came at once, my varied background had long allowed me ample options to witness the creative process at work. For years I appeared on top classical music rosters and traveled the world from my base in New York City. With a doctorate degree in Vocal Music Performance from the University of Michigan, my pedagogical training and qualifications assisted me to join faculty at an exclusive NYC Chelsea studio. The world's greatest entertainment professionals there honed the craft of singing and stagecraft. (The list of the school's former attendees included such names as Liza Minnelli, Alec Baldwin, Brooke Shields, Mandy Patinkin...)

My enduring interest in personal development and holistic wellbeing brought study with teachers and masters of time-honored traditions—even including a semester enrollment in an Oriental Medical School. These interests had begun before I arrived in NYC, which included training to black belt level in Okinawa Karate at a renowned dojo. It was in that dojo I first practiced Zen meditation.

Fascination with meditation and the so-called *internal arts* lead to study with a Korean monastic trained practitioner over a few years period in the Black Forest region of Germany. Continued interests in these arts continued through my life as I practiced Tai Chi, Chi Gung and found epic teachers. Keeping a trendy edge, in NYC I enrolled in entertainment and celebrity laden yoga classes.

With burgeoning interest in the Indian philosophic and spiritual tradition, fortune brought firsthand experience from the teachings of a modern Siddha master. This was what initially brought me on travels to south India. These varied explorations, along with courses and certifications in Western psychology and philosophy, world religion, success and manifestation training—more than I can remember—have all come together in my worldview.

Upon moving to New York City, one also often learns about other realities, and the importance of increasing financial intelligence. On practical fiscal matters, I delved into investing, financial markets, and real estate. I became licensed as a real estate agent in New York City and also worked in the field.

In 2012, as opportunity shifted, I transplanted to South Korea as a professor in South Korean universities, allowing more travel and direct access to the far East. After yearning for work in the business sector, I left university teaching and invested as a managing director in a South Korean firm. Together we brainstormed up a critically acclaimed restaurant in Seoul, South Korea.

Concurrently in this time, I kept up a singing career with concerts and participating in festivals. Delving deeper into broadcast, I boarded weekly flights back and forth from Seoul to Busan, to co-create for that time South Korea's only all English, all classical music radio show on the Busan English Radio (BEFM).

This kept my life flowing...along with the jungle trips...but we can keep those until a little later. I had wished for an active international life, and by so doing, garnered ample opportunities to learn. This was the soil in which the FLOW Laws developed and then suddenly came to the surface.

Potential

Vital to the FLOW Laws, is the idea of personal potential. In my conception for our subject at hand, potential is the ability to do or to have that which one truly wants.

The key word to this phrase is what one "truly" wants. Sometimes that which we genuinely want is obscured from ourselves. It can change, and even quickly. At times, unbeknownst to ourselves, it may be a principle we are reaching for more than one specific tangible goal. And this principle we are reaching for may allow various satisfying manifestations.

This concept will be touched on throughout the book, but as an introduction, I will give an example. Numerous individuals might simultaneously covet the title, president of the USA. However, there will only be one person at a time filling that position. Of course, one could approach string theory or extreme theoretical physics and thereby show various individuals to be president of the USA at the same time... But I will here stick with consensus reality that only one person can be USA president at a given moment.

Does this indicate then only one person can satisfy their dream of president in any given four year term? In a literal sense, yes. But examining what one truly wants—influence, a chance to be of service, you name it—it is my belief that one can find various expressions for a basic desire. The expression can be that which is most right for a person, and that fulfilling of the desire or goal can come fast.

When it comes down to it, past perceived power and prestige, the obligations and requirements of a position such as president may be more alluring in theory than in actuality. Thus, fulfilling potential is about working out the process. Our goals, or the fulfillment of our potential, keeps emerging with the fullness of time.

Living to full potential, one enters a dance of ambition. Ideas emerge, and the path shapes into the world of reality. Initial goals or destinations can change of course, as you get going, and this is ok. Follow along courses of action, clarify initial impulses, and see where it leads, even if it is different from originally intended. This is a fulfilling of potential, and sometimes it takes us by surprise.

A mystery and magic is the constant flux of our lives. This is a beautiful and awesome reality to grasp. A philosophy, such as you find in this book, garners stability through shifting circumstance. And as we grasp more the idea that success and personal potential is available for us to be fulfilled, it allows us freedom to enjoy other's success, as we know that success is not a limited phenomenon, and our success is also assured.

The process can be awe-inspiring, majestic even. Keep the course of the FLOW Laws as rudder to your life ship and it can navigate the way. When a ship sails out into uncharted waters there can come a "fear of God," grasping the immensity of potentials, of the universe itself. This can be overwhelming---even in its positivity. Take one step at a time, a solid philosophy and some added trust can turn anxiety into zest for being.

Get the ball rolling with the FLOW Laws! Life movement will show where your goals are taking you, this is co-creation with the world. Get the ball rolling and then adjust with the path. It may surprise you, what you find as you begin to live up to your potential—things might even be simpler than you thought.

Potential then, in this sense, is not only what you can do, but that which is fundamentally most right for you. If you really want something, there will be an expression available. Follow the path emergent or watch the path emerge, as it were. Follow the FLOW Laws.

Chalong Temple, Phuket, Thailand

Choices

On the famed resort island of Phuket in Thailand, a Thai friend and I once visited a renowned heritage temple. In a gilded hall in the temple there is an option to read your fortune. It is accomplished by separating a numbered stick from a bundle of other numbered wooden sticks. You take the number from your chosen stick and locate your corresponding fortune on tiny scrolls housed in an elaborate cupboard system.

Initially, not sure how to correctly choose the numbered stick, I randomly picked one. I searched my fortune by number and presented it to the friend. What a sour face he made! It was not a particularly good fortune. I considered for a moment and asked him, "Actually, how do you draw the numbered sticks?!"

We returned to the fortune telling chamber and I followed the rules of the hall. With a new number in hand, I again sought my fortune. His eyes popped wide, "Wow, this is a great prediction!"

My future was to a large part in my own hands, this declared to me. Was I going to put in the right effort? Investigate and follow the rules of the game? Or be content, come what may... Again, a choice.

The FLOW Laws offer you a choice. A choice to actively create your future, instead of living reactively—allowing your life to play out as always before. With these Laws, fulfill your potential, even allow for multiple possibilities of potential! Multiple meanings, paths—and even careers or business ventures—can happen simultaneously. Find your way to peak performance.

These concepts can help anyone, but if you wish extra counseling or need professional, personal, or medical assistance, seek the professional advice and assistance right for you. Highly successful people often have managers, advisors, therapists and coaches, etc....all a part of their team. This can be a part of your FLOW. This system is meant as an all-encompassing plan for existence. Initially, I thought to add extra details, from thoughts on diet, specific meditations and movements, to cosmology and even more considerations for growth. It became quickly clear that if I were to add all these aspects, the book would be outside the realm of streamline usability—which is a key point of the FLOW, Freedom Laws of the World ™.

Thus, along with the FLOW Laws, the 5 Modalities ™ series of courses and training was born. These modalities are modules containing steps and methods I have used for development, and compliment core principles in the FLOW Law System. The FLOW Laws stand alone, but if you want more ideas, more specifics, methods I have used in my own life, this can be found in the 5 Modalities series ™.

To further facilitate these systems of the FLOW Freedom Laws of the World ™ and the 5 Modalities ™ series I am developing seminars and training possibilities, including certifications for varying degrees of accomplishment. Another of my goals is to facilitate a resource structure incorporating information contained within this book.

There is something to be said of direct learning from an individual, either in seminar or in one on one training. Training with a qualified teacher in life-skills is a gift. For more information, please check out my company Apollo Naturopathics LLC's website at www.apollonatur.com.

For now, enjoy FLOW Freedom Laws of the World ™ and apply them to your life. Work with one law then move to the next. You do not need to *master* each law at once, but familiarize yourself with concepts, and move on.

As you become familiar with them, you can shift through them, even all within one session. Return to the law you need when the time is right. Regarding organization, the first three laws are linear in their approach (moving from one law directly to the next) and the last four are more conceptual.

This is a culmination blueprint for upgrading your existence. Congratulations on finding this...and let's get flowing!

PART II

FLOW Freedom Laws of the World ™

FLOW Law 1 – "Catch the Wave"

FLOW Law 2 – "Love the Wave"

FLOW Law 3 – "List the Wave"

FLOW Law 4 – "Time the Wave"

FLOW Law 5 – "Zen the Wave"

FLOW Law 6 – "Honor the Waves"

FLOW Law 7 – "Surf the Wave"

FLOW Law 1

"Catch the Wave"

The POINT of it all
Fix the existential question to free yourself for life
Zen of the sideways glance
Trust the FLOW
All in due time
A new adventure to engage the FLOW Laws
Meditation

"Catch the Wave" is an answer to the existential question. This law is the very point discussed with my waiter, who in the prologue, asked for the meaning of life. You need not seek an answer to the meaning of life, but rather connect into Life itself. Your involvement in life, from here and now going forward, is your meaning.

By acknowledging your connection to life, in the current moment, you find your meaning. This is the beginning to peace (and your direction) as well as a springboard to peak performance.

Wherever you are right now, accept yourself as a part of existence. It is ok if your emotions are not in line, or if you are dissatisfied with aspects of your life. This is normal and any emotions are catalysts for growth.

Connect with the idea you are a current of being, running in tandem with the greater world around you. And your FLOW, your life, will shape up to be more and more what you desire. This connection is all you need going forward, there is really nothing to explain.

Again, this is your basic meaning of life. This is the Alpha and Omega of the FLOW Law system. This will grant you peace. There is a "Way" for all things available from here and now, it is freeing and simple.

Reorient your mind from defining or searching for meaning. Give up searching for yourself—you are already found—it is just a matter of your depth of realization. Release pent-up thoughts or emotions of uncertainty, of unease or doubt. Getting excitement for life, or a sense of relief that things can get better, is key.

As with the waves of the ocean, you need not scientifically explain or *understand* a wave on the beach. You can just "Catch the Wave" and ride it into shore. In the same vein, you can locate thoughts or ideas, and with a current of excitement, sail to your desires in life.

As you associate more with the current of life and get excited with the process—more than any specific details—you will find trust and enjoyment in the process. And as you feel more trust in a general way, this will also flow into the specifics. You will find yourself freer to make new choices and move seamlessly in your path, and to enjoy this process of "Catch the Wave."

Waves on Marina Beach, Chennai, India

THE POINT OF IT ALL

All you need for your meaning, is to "Catch the Wave" of your life or FLOW, and keep doing it, thereby establishing your meaning—as relationship with existence. This grants philosophic freedom and peace of mind. Beyond this, imagine your wave carrying you to a generally positive or even specific future of your desire. If there is something you wish, there is a manifestation available, and a "wave" that can bring you there.

If you desire the *meaning of life*, this is an answer. If you need direction in a project, you can take a moment and "Catch the Wave." Check in with your life (or your "wave") and in all positivity trust for a best direction moving forward from right now. There is always a most efficient direction forward from the present moment, trust into its appearance.

We all get stuck in unproductive thoughts or states, we all become annoyed, or down. And if you have been long entrenched in various non-desirable emotional states, it can take some time to catch a new wave. Remember these states are shifting, the idea that there is a best-way-from-now-possible leading to your dream, can be freeing. And then by getting excitement into that idea, you can start to shake yourself loose from what is holding you back.

Let your mind go and notice the best idea or vision for your future that comes to you at the moment. This is a start, this idea can be a launch pad. Know there is a "wave" that can bring you there. This initial idea can be anything...from something to ponder, a specific action or direction, or even a thought for needed rest or just having a moment to feel your body.

If there is any actionable thought, follow this thought as far as you can, remember—there is a way to your potential, and it does not have to all happen at once. And to "Catch the Wave," you do not need to *feel* anything that extraordinary, you do not need any vast spiritual experience for it to be working.

"Catch the Wave" may grant a profound shift of consciousness, or it can be much more subtle. It might just be a momentary feeling of relaxation—or just being a bit more hopeful. Or you may not feel anything externally, but your subconscious may have gotten a hint. Even small adjustments can lead to profound change over time, with vast ramifications.

There is no judgement of you or your past action, it is your inspired movement from right now that counts. This is another aspect of hope infused in this law. There is always a *best* way forward for you no matter the circumstance. If something was missed on the way, release regret and "Catch the Wave."

The world is a mysterious place, there is always a best way to remedy absolutely anything. FLOW Law 1 is simple, but profound, do not underestimate its power. If I find myself ever in a position of doubt, or concern over ramifications from choices, FLOW Law 1 gets me back on track in a proactive way.

I have had some career options end for me prematurely, and I remember frustration and heavy emotion when all had not gone as planned. Along with it, I entertained anxiety for the future. However, soon I was about to "Catch the Wave" to new possibilities, even better than I had planned. Had I trusted this earlier, I could have accepted the initial change with more grace. I could have saved time realizing the change was simply the appearance of new scenarios for a better future.

"Catch the Wave" is a battle cry for the high achiever. As you realize all things you hope for have a *potential* manifestation available, you trust it. As you find peace and centeredness in this process, you harness the energy necessary to take confident action.

Stability of mind and body are necessary to maintain states of high activity and peak performance, as is a refined ability to stay on track. When new occurrences and situations develop, you need maneuverability to redirect your thoughts and actions calmly and skillfully into your best direction—and as fast as you can. When your life speeds up, you need to keep on with "Catch the Wave."

If you get angry on the way, or frustrated, that's ok too! You can turn any emotion towards encouragement to your goals. Emotions are energy, power...we can even call them potentiality. You can use all of them to inspire you! For me, I want to steer my emotional states towards a more fulling and enjoyable process. Fun of course, may at times take some focus. Remember, "Catch the Wave" is also a skill to hone.

Ultimately, you see that your enjoyment, or fulfillment, is not related to any one external creation or accomplishment. Your joy lies in the connection to and the pleasure of this system—and of Life itself.

"Catch the Wave," is not only an answer to vast questions of life, such as in the experience set in the introduction, but also a formula to re-center and redirect yourself in daily life. Here's a simple example of "Catch the Wave" in motion...

One evening around eight or nine o'clock after dinner an espresso was offered to me, and I accepted. As I was trying to sleep a few hours later, I realized suddenly, that for this night, coffee might not have been the best idea. I started to feel regret about this, and I immediately caught myself, and checked into my "wave."

I realized that even if I did not sleep well, I could do some meditation during the night. And if I needed, I did have time for a nap the next afternoon. This "Catch the Wave" moment allowed me to relax more in the "current" situation. And I ended up sleeping better than I would have, had I not caught onto this new stream of thought.

This first FLOW Law is practical, but perhaps most philosophical in nature of the laws. Coming up, we will look at this law from various angles, but still based on the two basic premises of the law. The first, how the idea as a philosophy is geared to finding peace of mind. And next, how this relates into freeing yourself for positive actions, up to that state of peak performance.

FIX THE EXISTENTIAL QUESTION TO FREE YOURSELF FOR LIFE

First, we will continue with this idea of FLOW Law 1 as a peace giving, philosophical answer. The idea of finding "a" or "the" meaning of life is very tied up with the concept of being human. Even from humanity's earliest literature, the quest for meaning played a vital role. One of these earliest of stories, is that of Gilgamesh. To summarize, in this story we find the character of Gilgamesh, who loses a best friend. The friend happens to be a kind of half-beast—we will not get into all the details here—but the point is, as Gilgamesh faced loss, he went on this very type of quest to find meaning.

This question of meaning is deep in the human psyche and may be affecting us more than we sometimes appreciate. It can be a nagging idea or feeling that we might somehow be missing something. And this very question or feeling may itself be the reason of actually missing out on a fuller experience.

Most of us do not aim to be a philosopher, but we do need frameworks to guide our lives, and it can be hard or even impossible to ever definitely ascertain if our life is a "success" or "on the right track." So, in this law we let go of this question, which is not serving us, and we focus on the FLOW.

Beyond assisting with existential uncertainty, this first FLOW Law or "Catch the Wave" allows development of plans of actions or intent. And the combined FLOW Laws give a support or structure to move forward with confidence. As you find more peace of mind overall, you will find more options to act and have the confidence to do it.

In life we need a structure to work with. I remember when I began studying singing, some teachers would say, "Relax, and just do it!" And it is a great idea, but only if you have some framework. This book, this practical philosophy, is "real world" advice for that framework.

Using "Catch the Wave"–along with the combined seven Laws—as you find your peace, you will be simultaneously finding specific ways to implement your creative focus to direct your personal resources toward the life you want. And this process becomes a compass for life, a compass is a simple tool but can have a huge impact on navigating a course.

When my restaurant waiter came to me for a meaning of life, there was the implication that he was missing it. Despite his fun, charm, and the basically good-natured interaction, when pressed, when being *honest* with himself, there was apparently a hole he felt in his personal experience. Now you have a premise to fix or fill in this hole yourself.

ZEN OF THE SIDEWAYS GLANCE

Delving in and thinking about our life situations, about our plans of actions for our futures, is valid and useful. However, it can quickly move from useful thinking to overthinking, and then even to anxiety. As you "Catch the Wave," toss out the less useful varieties of "over thinking." Get into the idea of the "Zen of the sideways glance."

For a long time, I have thought if I were to establish a meditation school, I would call it the "Zen of the sideways glance."

This is the concept of turning your mind away from thoughts, which might even be true, but which are not serving you.

Here is a simple example. Let's say you are coming to the end of a great beach vacation, and you start to feel "low" or "down" about that. Just ignore the reality—which is not serving you—and enjoy your time. This allows you a method to change focus, and this is one example of the "Zen of the sideways glance." It is not to discount reality, but simply to glance at the less enjoyable reality as necessary, and then move on with thoughts which fulfill.

There is a possibility to lose good time worrying about "realities." If we look at certain realities of life too intensely it can even be overwhelming. Instead of facing loss, impermanence, or change directly on—or having too much focus on worries—get into the "Zen of the sideways glance" and then "Catch the Wave." There is always a most fun and efficient way to life. Catch your moment available right now—and let that lead you to your steps and actions.

If you attempt to grasp mentally all of life—or figure it all out in overly complex details—it can burden you and freeze ability for actions—actions you are capable of and which will bring results you want. "Zen of the sideways glance" lets you manage or choose your focal reality, and then "Catch the Wave" to your goal. Life is bigger than we are, it is not our job to get caught up trying to figure it all out, on a philosophical level, or even on much more personal levels.

Employ "Catch the Wave" with the "Zen of the sideways glance!" Work skillfully in your path with the information you have now. As you find more peace with existence, you will be more available for answers and actions you need.

TRUST THE FLOW

A theory of how all this works, which I entertain, basically goes as follows. The process of trust into "Catch the Wave" is cumulative, you will naturally begin to develop more trust as you continue in the process. Along with sense of trust, comes energy or excitement that will inspire you to take action or "movement." As you start having actions and success from them, this cycle of belief and trust continues growing. As you drop worries and unnecessary thought, your thinking "streamlines," becomes more stable and focused, and may even connect to a deeper thinking or to your subconscious.

As this deeper thinking integrates, different aspects or varying physical parts of the brain or body may "think" for you. This may be a tap into thinking beyond the rational mind. By creating a practice of "Catch the Wave" you may access deeper thoughts or an intuitive mind, perhaps even aspects of the subconscious that almost seem to have a knowledge of its own.

In a rudimentary way, I see (minimally) two sides of that coin which is the "mind." A rational and then an intuitive or deeper mind. The longer you work with this type of FLOW system, the more trust and positivity you will garner in your life. The theory continues that as you do so, the more you can tap into your deeper understanding. In the end what is most important is not exactly how "Catch the Wave" functions for you, but that it does function to free you for more ease and success.

We always must choose priorities, but then quickly the question can arise, "Did we make right choices?" Another aspect of trust relates to focusing less on if a choice was "correct" in the past, and more on what is the best course of action into the future. Worry less, and place consideration on your actions from the present situation forward.

I am often traveling, and my life simultaneously runs in different places, even in various countries around the world. There is my life in Asia, in the US, my music career, my business involvements... Sometimes I find myself in a city or hotel room and catch myself thinking...should I have decided to come here? Would have it been better to follow up with a different pursuit?

Now, as much as possible, I consciously throw out thoughts of "Did I make the right decision!" This is an exceedingly comforting practice! I trust there is something for me (to do, to learn, to be) right where I am. This brings better sleep too, knowing where I am is good. And especially with the internet, we can do many things remotely—wherever we may find ourselves.

In the end, no one can tell us if we did the "right" thing. But by loving where you are in life as much as you can, whatever state that may be, and by staying sensitive, you can be increasingly confident in an inner guidance. What if you do not believe in an inner guidance? Honestly, is there much alternative?!

I make a choice to believe in inner guidance. Will *not sleeping* because maybe you made a wrong choice help anything? Probably not. By proactive thought and actions, overcoming thoughts of doubt and concern, there is the most potential to fulfill your desires.

"Catch the Wave" can bring you into an intuitive state of trust. It might even feel your FLOW knows your desires or wishes more than you do. You can start to allow your FLOW to give you what you need in its own time.

Author taking a moment in Shanghai, China

ALL IN DUE TIME

Now let us briefly consider our FLOW in time. This is another aspect we can consider for a sense of peace, ease, or release. And this sense of relaxation of mind, or peace, as we are here discussing it, is vital.

We are—or for the most part we are—experiencing life in a basically linear reality. Time moves for us in a line. We wake up in the morning, have breakfast, do whatever it is we do, then there is lunchtime. It is not breakfast and lunch simultaneously in our experience. So then, life has an order to it for us and we are doing one thing after another.

We basically all have a consensus we experience reality one thing at a time. However, there are times, we want to see *all* our desires fulfilled immediately. This can be something like, enjoying breakfast and lunch at the same time. Now having things get done fast is great, and I want to see my goals achieved in good time. However, sometimes we create unrealistic expectations.

We can find peace allowing different experiences to unfold in time with one following the other. This idea is most helpful for the over-achiever who is never satisfied. Being "never satisfied" certainly has its upside, it draws us forward to new success. However, the downside is equally obvious, never being satisfied.

Thus, one aspect of learning to trust in the FLOW, is to also trust that Life can bring us our fulfillment, when the time is right. This requires we enjoy the aspects of life—as they come along. We can actively remind ourselves of this to heighten our awareness to the good things around us all the time. As we do this, we can look forward to that which is to come, but still enjoy the time we are in.

A NEW ADVENTURE TO ENGAGE THE FLOW LAWS

As you embrace these new concepts, the change in mindset might feel profound. But little by little, you can comprehend the process and simultaneously give your mind relief. You can drop unnecessary constrictions that hold you back, and the process becomes easier and easier.

This law can also be applied as a pictorial image. As I love the ocean, I sometimes imagine being caught up in a beautiful, crested wave that takes me where I want to go. Fast and easy. If this image is useful for you, go with the FLOW.

Life is intricate and complicated, like the mechanisms of a mechanical clock or watch. The wheels may seem separate, but they are all interconnected. As you feel a release in one aspect of your life—be it in a broader philosophical approach or in the specifics of daily events—this release will have ramifications across all aspects of your life.

It may seem self-evident, to "Catch the Wave" or go with the FLOW, but the most self-evident truths can be missed, by the very nature of their simplicity. And with this, we prepare to FLOW into the second Law.

As you "Catch the Wave" you can find more and more reason—even a necessity! —to feel good. You might think that "feeling good" is not serious—but keep reading.

Law 1 is the framework on which the other laws are based. As you keep on finding new "centeredness," with "Catch the Wave" Flow Law 1, the balanced arrangement of the FLOW Freedom Laws of the World ™ will arrange themselves for your best interest. The process is cumulative, as you find your being, you realize your meaning.

MEDITATION
I embrace this idea that grants freedom. By resting and resetting into this moment, I release any need to search for a meaning, as my meaning is in my connection to Life. It is right here, right now, and leading me to my best future.

FLOW Law 2

"Love the Wave"

Build up good feelings and get connected
Go ancient
Feeling good is responsible and a process
Wellness starts and is based on feeling well
Engaged work as a manifestation of positivity
Success is transferable
Meditation

    Having a motivated mindset, with stamina and enjoyment, is one of the best ways to reach potential and to hook into your goals and best life! The second FLOW Law will get you inspired and moving. The premise is any excitement for life you can foster is beneficial. Not only are specific goals useful, but so is fostering a general attitude of positivity—and using all means available to get your energy "revved-up." Finding an emotional state of eagerness, more than any specific goals (which comes later in FLOW Law 3), you create an atmosphere to get your life set on "GO!"

    As your experience with the FLOW continues, you use emotion as motivator and barometer. That is, as your life experience becomes more enjoyable, this encourages you to apply the FLOW principles even more, and as you do so, the virtuous cycle convinces you that you are on the right track. Apply this to all aspects of your life!

FLOW Law 1 may have convinced you of the benefits of "Catch the Wave." You may be excited to jump into this daring practice and create more flowing realities, and by doing so, watch new meanings appear for your life...

Law 2 further answers, *"How do I find this FLOW?"*

"Love the Wave" is concerned with two basic premises. First, cultivate as much enjoyment in your current situation as possible—along with enthusiasm for upcoming experiences. And second, consistently switch perspective from viewing what appears to be life challenges to be opportunities for creativity.

This book is a philosophical approach to life, not a fitness or financial planner, nor a "how to guide" to a perfect partner. Though employing these principles, you can transform yourself into a person who will increase health, wealth, and attract other people. Each of these laws functions to develop aspects of your being. "Love the Wave" is the next decisive step.

BUILD UP GOOD FEELINGS AND GET CONNECTED

To develop anything, to maintain anything, you need to garner enthusiasm for the project—be it for that relationship, investment, or for anything else in life. With a build-up of energy, excitement, and enthusiasm, you can determine what it is you desire and how to strive towards it...get revved up!

So, let's start out by ramping up appreciation at every angle! At this point, it does not matter what brings excitement...just find a way to create a baseline of positivity in your days. Building up positivity is an investment in your future, and a method to create the energy or momentum to catch (or create) more powerful waves of life.

One starting place is to notice and enjoy the senses at your disposal; to see, sense, feel, taste, smell or hear. Enjoy the tasks of your life, the mundane even. Enjoy the idea of enjoying! Purposely enjoy the minutes when you have a short break. You can even enjoy the water washing your hands! It might sound banal, but water feels great. These are all secrets to refresh your mind as quickly as possible.

Finding enjoyment now—even before life changes—is one of the best ways to inspire change. Moods may feel immobile, but it is amazing how malleable and resilient we as humans can be. Work consciously on this process until you hit the subconscious with it. That is, keep practicing consciously, repeating these ideas until this state of underlying enjoyment feels more automatic. It is an on-going process, but it does get easier. And keep trusting, you and your life are acceptable right now, and life need not have been different.

It is straightforward, when we feel good, we have more energy. When we feel good, we get things done. When we feel good, more people will want to be around us. What is holding us back from squeezing as much enjoyment—as an exercise—out of every aspect of our lives that we can?!

Basically, we have doubts. "Will I have stamina to keep going?" "Will the steps work for me?" "I have tried to feel excited in the past and it did not work out." "My life is not that exciting, why should I feel excited!?"

These are thoughts and questions that do not serve. Until we try new forms, formulas, and actions—and stick with it—we cannot discover how far we will go. My premise is we all can find lasting change, and a spirit of excitement is an emotional starting place to find exciting, new thoughts. Do not wait for your life to change to appreciate it! Appreciate now, and then watch the changes develop.

And along the way, do not worry if your mind, body or emotions are not in a "feel good" state. Besides, concern does not help you feel good! Give yourself a margin of error. Perfection is not always practical to shoot for and we do not always get the results we initially expected. You will never ultimately "get there," so you do not need to worry about not being there.

Another obvious point, you need not be in a good mood or feel 100 percent to get things done, this is natural. Anxiety, for instance, can be a wonderful motivator towards achievement. Any less "enjoyable" emotions can inspire you to action. But for peace of mind and working your way to peak performances, this principle of "Love the Wave," creates more ideal states. Employ it as much as you can, it is a tool.

Most crucial in life and in projects, is often that initial surge of energy to get things started. By ramping up your energy and convincing yourself of your passion, you can get a project started. When the ball of one's life starts rolling, the magic of the world can awaken specific ideas for you and opportunities arise faster.

As momentum picks up, the effect is cumulative. The world around you will have more influence to reach you, or you will be more available for assistance, to find your direction. It can even seem; Life starts to give clues and help push or roll the ball of your life along the way.

There are a lot of simple things to "up" our energy and motivation. Changes in our lives do not have to be monumental, small changes are cumulative. "Love the Wave," build resolve and stamina, and accumulate your energy and FLOW. One simple example of lifting my mood, especially useful when I sit down to write, is that I turn on up-beat classical music.

I am a fan of the Bach keyboard concerti. This is very subjective, what music or activities brings enjoyment or inspiration, but when I hear the dynamic rhythm and pulse of Bach, this inspires me. Contained in this chapter is a multitude of information on how to "Love the Wave." How you create your own atmosphere is personally up to you.

I constantly seek enjoyment to feel lighter and more up-beat. Throughout the day I look for points that feel optimistic or exciting to me. Remember, it does not always matter the nature of the specific thoughts, most valuable can often simply be the state of positivity and readiness for actions that results.

This desire for a high energy, up-beat state is partially resulting from my ambition to get things done. Then, because of this ambitious character, I want to see things get done fast. Which is a useful trait, but I can also feel "stuck" or frustration when things are not unfolding as fast or "on track" as I would hope. The answer? Change perspective. This is the second aspect of "Love the Wave."

When faced with frustration, as quick as possible engage creativity. Remind yourself that one's stress is another's puzzle. If I say to myself, "Love the Wave," it is a codeword to change mental direction. Higher functioning people may not necessarily have less issues to deal with, it is that higher functioning individuals work skillfully in complex environments. Learn to orient your mind to find new opportunities considering your current developments.

With new perspective, we can better view our challenges as something to work out, as a part of the process. We often desire "completion" and would rather "irritating steps" go away. Rewire your mind to best address challenges. Reorient your thinking and attempt enjoyment at any given moment. It is a part of gratitude. This constant game of Flow Law 2, as simple as it may sound, is also a skill to hone. A puzzle can be fun.

GO ANCIENT

Ancient systems or philosophies are attractive as methods of cultivation for health and well-being. The idea something lasted so long gives substance to it. Opportunities available to us that touch on historic perspective—or at least the "idea" of the traditional—span from yoga classes, movement or dance systems, various meditations, massage, martial arts, or many other art forms. I have explored many such methods.

Traditional park, Beijing, China

Favorite memories spring from my graduate school period discovering advanced Tai Chi and Chi Gung with master, Gabriel Chin. He gave firsthand access to innumerable techniques and ideas from the world of Chinese martial arts, exercise, meditation—and Chi Gung. For those not familiar, Chi Gung is often described as breathing, stretching, or "energy" exercises, often related to meditation. Tai Chi as such, can even be considered a form of Chi Gung.

Gabriel kept a distinctive style, resembling the appearance of a Chinese sage, with an aura of mastery. His encyclopedic understanding of traditional Chinese systems enormously impressed, as did his quickness, wit and personal style at description and demonstration. Also, being an excellent chef, especially competent at pulling together dishes from varying regions across China, there might even have come along an occasional concise culinary allusion.

Once I was attempting comprehension of boundaries of thought amongst varying traditional philosophical systems. I remember grappling with distinctions in philosophical holdings between varying groups, such as certain ideas held between Daoists or Buddhists. He turned to me in this hopeless quandary of mine and took care of considerations quickly.

"Don't worry too much about it, it's all soup-like," he said. "Dishing out" a summary of his view that—especially amongst the Chinese canon of philosophy and practice—ideas or techniques could be shared among varying groups—blurring from one system to the next. And depending on time, place, and spirit of the day, in a very practical sense, in any given group—all was up in the air anyway! In essence, defining a "comprehensively-correct-traditional-understanding" of basically anything was from unlikely to impossible—because it had always been mixed up like soup!

There is no way to touch on the legacy of Gabriel Chin in this volume. However, within the "soup-like" enormity of philosophy, exercise, and meditations we did together, I can ascertain a common denominator. In those practices, there included a resulting sense of well-being in body and mind. Cultivating a sense of "connectedness" within oneself, within one's life and in tandem with the world at large.

Gabriel would say, "Connect between heaven and earth." This included a sensation of connection and ease in the body from top of head to feet. We practiced using our attention to bring the mind, and then the "chi" (life energy), to different vital points in the system. Letting the energy settle in the body, it allowed a comfortable feeling to sink, especially into the lower abdomen. This would in turn also prove to be beneficial for digestion. Bringing this practice further, energy could be "sunk" to the feet, giving a feeling of being "grounded," and better in contact with the earth.

There were many different practices, but the fundamental idea was to foster a state of balance, homeostasis, and ultimately good health. In relation to the FLOW System, it is finding that good feeling state, or to "Love the Wave." Though this state should be natural, that which is most "natural," however, can elude us. Think of the art of acting, being asked to read a script "naturally," can be challenging. Thus, it is worthwhile to pursue practices, including "Love the Wave," that assist to bring about this connection into the "natural" state of balance.

Convince yourself that you have some control of your mental and emotional states, that connectedness is easy—and you will be ahead. This is just a taste of exercise and ideas that will also be found in the 5 Modalities ™ methods for cultivation. However, the underlying concept, "Love the Wave" is simple. I am grateful to master Gabriel Chin, and many teachers and friends who have helped me on my way. Gratitude is another means to "Love the Wave."

FEELING GOOD IS RESPONSIBLE AND A PROCESS

Often "getting down to business" or "getting serious" implies sobriety—even an antithesis to a good time. I want accomplishment in as "fun" way as possible. You *can* pin-point focus on a goal—along with an energized good feeling mood. High performance, and serious intent, can be accomplished with great enjoyment, and in my book, go hand in hand. Pointedly, to keep a high-performance state for extended periods, without burn-out, keeping the mood up and light is paramount. It is responsible to feel good. Take "feeling good" seriously!

That said, your demeanor should match your current environment, with a clear focus on the task at hand. Maintain balance, and rapport with others is a part of the process. In a board room for an important meeting, I would want to match the prevailing attitude. However, an underlying thought of "now the real fun is about to begin" can spark a flame of productivity. That is "Love the Wave."

If you are upping your productivity level, especially on big projects, you may find yourself occasionally tired, at your limit, or even exhausted. This is normal in intense high performances situations. But how do you view your exhaustion? Are you a champion extending your limit and growing? Or are you a victim to circumstance?

It takes a strong mind to overcome boundaries and build up your mental and physical stamina to the next level. That is where the power of "Love the Wave," can come in. As challenges arise, you keep perspective on the bright and productive side.

It is not that we are "playing pretend" in "Love the Wave." Pretending that our circumstances are different than reality or creating unreal perception of our situation—rosy illusions for as long as the bubble lasts. This law is about how to arrange direction of focus...keep getting into productive thoughts! And certainly, bad behavior or sloppiness from yourself or others has no place in the FLOW. Send that on a wave out the door.

Use this law as an alchemy for heavy emotions, transform them to lighter, and proactive emotions. If you are feeling anger or frustration, imagine that there is a power or "steam" behind that emotion. And then by thinking that emotion is a pent-up expression of your desire for achievement, you can transform that emotion into motivation.

If "stuck," say to yourself, you feel stuck because of your passion—and passion is a useful energy. Working your way through this process is personal. However, by rearranging our views on our emotional states, we can find "taking-off" places to new brighter futures.

Even though you may not have control over all happenings in your life, you can control your responses. The more you consciously arrange your mind, the better results can be expected, and the less you will let individual disappointments affect you. If for some reason, you cannot move around a certain blockage, or need assistance, you can again, always approach professional help in counseling or therapy. Seeing a professional can expedite the way.

In time, you will gravitate to more empowering thoughts, instead of being pushed around by your emotions. Getting serious about "feeling good" is a beneficial goal for a high achiever, and "Love the Wave" goes beyond mere enthusiasm. It removes *dis-ease*, and through the garnering of feelings of well-being, creates a foundation for health.

WELLNESS STARTS AND IS BASED ON FEELING WELL

When we are healthy and our bodies are functioning well, we literally feel well. There is a correlation between thoughts of well-being and actually *being* healthy. Attitude and clearer mind can bring a sense of health, as we start to feel grateful for life in general, and this can have cumulative results.

You take energy from thoughts about problems, get into enthusiasm, and you feel better. As you feel better, you have more energy to take care of yourself. If it is exercise or food choices or following up with the right health care providers. It is a virtuous cycle. Smile into yourself and your possibilities as much as you can.

We often feel if a problem comes up, especially about our health, we must dwell in the severity of it. This is natural, as our health is our life. But there is that oxymoron, the more we spend energy concerning ourselves about our problems, the more we can be occupied by them.

This results in part from our training to look for malfunction in a system, and this is, of course, vital for our lives functioning. In our jobs, our families, our health, we need to determine the problem areas and address them. But there comes a limit in this "problem identifying" mentality, when it becomes actually more beneficial to dwell a bit in the emotional satisfaction of what is well-functioning. By reducing our stress levels in general, and thus feeling better, our physical organism has a better chance to take care of itself.

Clearly, it can be a challenge to deal with health issues or chronic conditions. But positive attitudes and emotion can adjust your brain / body chemistry to your advantage. See your physician when needed, follow up on any treatment, and in the meantime, keep the spirit and "Love the Wave."

When studying piano in Germany, I developed a small cyst or nodule on one of my fingers. It concerned me mildly, and when I met one of my friends' fathers—who was an award-winning physician in Germany and head of an important clinic—he told me something I never forgot.

He gave the German verb, *ignorieren*, "to ignore." He said to me, sometimes regarding these small issues in our body, the best mindset is to ignore them. Having his permission to ignore it, I did. I completely forgot about this issue, and perhaps a month later it came to my mind, I checked, and it was gone.

When we feel good, we can have spontaneous relief of physical symptoms. When we feel good, our digestion will function more effectively, which is vital to absorb energy from food and fuel our systems. This is another virtuous cycle of health.

We have such great health care in comparison to say 100 years ago, sometimes it can be hard to know the limits of modern medicine, and when the innate wisdom of the human body can take over. There can be issues of over-attending to health when the best process is to "Love the Wave," involve in life, and allow the body to take care of itself. Certainly, have a great health team! Find the professionals you trust and create a plan. Once this is together, then get into thoughts that fire you up about living as best you can. The most powerful cure and maintenance of health, in the end, can come from your own zest for life.

Share D Table restaurant, Seoul, South Korea

ENGAGED WORK AS A MANIFESTATION OF POSITIVITY

The words "thought manifestation" certainly relate to "Catch the Wave." An implication of the idea may seem to "get things done" without a change in yourself—simply by thinking—say perhaps while in the comfort of your living room, just with your thoughts. Now there may be some truth to this. However, following up from "Catch the Wave" and in preparation of Law 3 (the point at which we identify specific goals) remember, "Love the Wave" will most likely ultimately inspire you to take actionable steps to make things happen!

After I left teaching at the university in Korea, I wanted to try something new. I wanted to open a business and for a long time had the idea of opening a restaurant. Many celebrities open restaurants, this idea fired me up and sounded exciting. I used "Love the Wave" to ramp up excitement, and ready myself for the plans to come.

Investing in a foreign corporation was a first big step, along with creating a business structure with my partners and creative team. Then came finding the location, renovating the venue, and all the steps in opening a trendy and largescale, open-concept market style venue. All the while working in what was still not my native country (or language)—it was destined to be one of the bigger waves I had encountered.

If we think of projects as waves, they can come in a variety of levels. A small wave might be the excitement to clean up your apartment for an afternoon. Depending on the size (and state) of your apartment that could be a bigger wave!

With our restaurant endeavor, we knew it would be a big wave to ride, and we jumped in when we felt the time was right. We pulled it together quickly, it was exciting, and we had a fast, great success. We had days with lines forming outside the restaurant. This was also taking place in a challenging period in recent Korean history, with a lot of political changes happening. Our restaurant was a celebration of fun and life in Seoul.

It was a time of great excitement, but it was a huge wave, and it was not exactly easy. In hindsight, I would have done certain things differently, but I learned a lot. "Love the Wave" does not indicate everything will remain easy and manageable, life can get big and exciting...and even scary. As you put more "juice" into your life, the stakes will get higher and experience can get heated up—such as when you turn up the flame in an international market restaurant.

That is when these FLOW Laws are most important to apply, "Love the Wave!", especially as life shows challenges and the waves get bigger. The more intensity rises, the more you need to rise to the occasion. Find the positive, and then stay in that positive leaning mode. As you do so, and keep following a proactive course, you become a new person in the process.

The more you keep your wits about you in high energy circumstances, the more you can skillfully manage your manifestation. And you can even steer off—or duck under— a wave that is too much for you to handle. Use "Love the Wave" to stay on track.

SUCCESS IS TRANSFERABLE

In the Asian philosophy of Daoism, if a person masters an art or skill, he is said not only to learn that specific skill or way, but to some extent a more general *Way* of how to approach life. Success is transferable. As you succeed to "Love the Wave" in one part of your life, you can *love* it in another!

It is no coincidence that in countries such as Japan, different arts have etymological similarities. Examples such as tea ceremony (chadō), training in sword work (kendō), the way of karate or the "empty hand," (karate dō), all end with "dō"—which can be translated as the "Way." These differing arts and skills have an interrelation or correlation in that all are paths, or *Ways* of being. As one grows in one path, one will ultimately understand the interrelations of many, or all paths.

Also, as you "Love the Wave" you are keeping your mind "light." By looking to enjoyable aspects or "lightness" of even challenging times, you will find capacity for more ease and ultimately success and maneuverability into the future. You will have more options to find the assistance which the world has to offer.

In my mind, keeping the *Way* light, is one of the concepts of success—that can be transferable. Here is a short story on "Love the Wave" and accessing the "lightness" and "light" emotions, that I see as one of the keys of success.

A path or "Way" leading around Shuri Castle, Naha city, Okinawa, Japan

Martial arts have been a passion and hobby of mine. Physical training has many benefits and can be life-changing on its own. During graduate school, I heard of a seminar by a veteran trainer / coach to various famous martial arts stars, including to movie star Jet Li. Along with this coach came another Chinese martial arts national champion... I signed up for this seminar in a heartbeat.

Practicing with the group, I received a "thumbs-up" from the coach—which made my day. Meeting this national champion, he noticed I enjoyed training in the martial arts and had some experience. And upon learning I am a musician, he was eager to talk about the similarities of the various arts. We spoke about developing skill-sets, especially performance-based skills, such as required in music and martial arts. While having this discussion of "Ways," this Chinese national champion opened up with me regarding his philosophy of life and training.

Before we parted, he left me with these words. "My *Way* is, be light—and work hard! Be light, work hard!!" It felt as if he gave me his best wishes with those words. When you are light, in a good mood, you get the most done. Not only your mood, but your physical body will feel lighter, and with this lightness, without getting weighed down, you can achieve your greatest impact in your endeavors.

The more energy you create with "Love the Wave," the more energy you will have to make and enjoy your success, whatever that may mean to you. And there is something mystical about success, the more you attract it, the more it seems attracted to you.

Ultimately, success is a personal and subjective experience. I will venture to say that a meaningful life can have as many forms as there are individuals to experience it. If we decide the meaning of life can be found in a resourceful involvement in Life at this very moment, then "Catch the Wave," directly to "Love the Wave."

More importantly than any future benefit, enjoyment and satisfaction in the present can change your life right now. The more you sink into this optimistic, forward looking, "ground state," the more you can turn this experience of Earth into one of riding the wave. You then flow with your dreams—like a thrilled surfer—as opposed to being tossed around by the waves of life.

MEDITATION
Pleasure in life, joy in my unfolding and co-creating with the world, is not only acceptable, but tantamount for my well-being and success. Choosing self-perpetuating good feeling, the magic of life will right at this very moment begin to influence my future.

FLOW Law 3

"List the Wave"

Organize your mind with a 3-step process

-Create a catchword
-Initiate mid to long-range actionable plans
-Set a daily and weekly schedule

Organize your life, living space, and dress for success
Organize your financial mind
Organize into creativity
See where the FLOW leads
Meditation

 As you began the Flow System, you freed up your mind for possibilities, and you began to unlock your energy. In the third Law you move from theoretical and conceptual into practical and actionable steps. In Law 2 we created energy in an all-purpose way and now we discover more specific outlets for our enthusiasm.

 In Law 3, by listing and organizing your goals (and organizing your life in general) you will gain clarity. By starting from general ideas and catchwords, and moving into action-oriented goals and plans, you organize your mind and thoughts around these benchmarks. This also compounds the everlasting pursuit to positivity as you uncover more specific passions.

Most of us have conscious-level plans or goals, ranging from general to specific. Aspirations vary from finding more happiness, to attracting a relationship, securing a job, or having better health—or something even more particular. After reading the first FLOW Laws you may be convinced potential is not only possible to fulfill, but practically assured if you follow the steps. In Law 3 you focus your mind and energy around specific goals—and allow Life to churn out the details in a unique and personal way.

You will follow tangible steps to your dreams awakening, however, you probably did not imagine all the steps before you began the process. Watching steps develop is a kind of magic in itself, as is the creative process. As inspiration and excitement appear, as if from out of the air, that energy helps carry to completion projects and goals...this is another form of magic.

ORGANIZE YOUR MIND WITH A 3-STEP PROCESS

Encompassing zest for life, organize your mind and bring desire to the surface in direct plans of action. Follow a 3-step process. 1. Uncover goals or states of being you wish to embrace and form them as catchwords to "spin" in your mind. 2. Determine broad plans and initiatives. 3. Create specific daily or weekly goals.

FLOW LAW 3

LIST 1 -- CATCHWORD:

MOVIE STAR

LIST 2--

READ FLOW BOOK –THIS MONTH
START YOGA CLASS–IN 2 WEEKS
WATCH ACTING VIDEOS–3 PER WEEK

LIST 3 --TODAY!!

DAILY ACTIVITIES PLUS....
FINISH READING FLOW LAW 3 !!
SEARCH AND ENROLL IN YOGA CLASS !!

Example of FLOW Law 3, 3-step process

1. Create a catchword

As you organize your mind and thoughts, begin with creating a "catchword" or phrase that encapsulates your goal. Start by finding general concepts which inspire you and latch onto these ideas. If specific ideas come up, use those. What do you really want to have or be? Don't worry if your plan seems farfetched! Is it a *movie star* existence? Is it a better relationship? Is it a glamorous life? Is it an increase in wealth, health, or being a more balanced and wiser person?

Before you consider inspired action, or judge it, just think for a moment what it is you might like and be honest with yourself. Maybe the ideas arising for you are relatively simple, such as "to be appreciated"? Ideas might appear to be an "organized person" or to have a more comfortable living space? What would you like? By simply choosing a catchword, such as "movie star," and repeating it to yourself, you might quickly feel a change. Even your body metabolism might react and improve with this simple change of mind—with visible results in how you feel and look. Keeping an inspired principle in your mind can change you in mysterious ways!

Feel good about your focal points. Objectives might be new, or they might solidify something already operational in your life. Form your images into a catchword that can electrify you!

This catchword is time sensitive; it is what is right for you now. It is memorable and places your mind and emotions in a distinct direction. This step creates the direction, and specific steps will be approached as you proceed.

By setting a direction in "List the Wave," you expand "Love the Wave" as you now are taking that excitement for life and directing it into a more defined objective—even if not yet too specific. This direction can commence a sense of purpose, confidence, and peace of mind, since now a process has been started. And of course, you are getting on track towards high performance, because your life and goals are lining up.

Finding one key idea to work on at a time might be a good start. Normally, to stay on track, I limit myself to at most three primary ideas in the same period. You can use as many as you wish, but the more catchwords you utilize, there is the issue with keeping focus.

If you are not exactly sure of your goals, get to general ideas, and start playing with them. One example from my life, was to become a "motivational resource." I kept thinking and spinning this idea and it refined itself as a concept into more energized phrases as I began developing the FLOW system. I realized that employing the FLOW principles to an apex of skill would require—and develop—mastery. Thus, I started spinning the apex of my system, "FLOW Master ™" —which has genuine ring to it.

From thinking in a general direction, in this 1st list, ideas start to flow. You will follow up on these ideas here in Law 3 "List the Wave," as part of the upcoming 2nd list. To be a "FLOW Master ™," I investigated and researched, took courses and visited more experts, learning new skills and integrating knowledge. It led to exotic travel and ultimately to writing this book—along with organizing seminars and programs. Spinning the catchwords created excitement and energy and from there the steps emerged.

Use this 1st list for big-picture concepts, and write them down, keeping the phrases short, concise, and inspiring. Stabilize these ideas in your consciousness, and as the full process integrates, you can move on to new ideas.

Moving to New York City, I felt passionate to cultivate a professional career as a classical singer. It is a niche, competitive field, so I was consistently spinning ideas such as "opera star," "opera bass," or "classic rock star." I attempted to keep it fun, to keep it light...and to keep the dream! There was ample to occupy my mind and time, but this overarching thought assisted my life and actions to revolve around these goals.

You want to employ phrases that energize you, phrases that can wake you in the morning and see you through the day. Waking with "opera star," I kept this idea in my mind throughout the day, assisting me to stay on track and create actionable plans (which we will discuss in list two.)

And for me, life did move quickly once I arrived in NYC. Within two weeks, I discovered the academy in NYC where I became faculty for several years, and I started singing professional engagements after a few months. It was encouraging. Then after winning a prize in an international competition, I landed my first agent, or as referred to in the classic music field, a manager.

However, this specific manager was soon transitioning his career into a related arts field. Around a year thereafter, I was again on the hunt for new representation. I realized quickly, I needed excellent management to make things happen the way I wanted. The catchword "top management" appeared, with related permutations including "star management," or "world class representation."

Giving myself small incentives, I kept spinning ideas along. In Central Park there is a picturesque bridge I strolled by almost daily. I decided to walk around it until I secured my new management. I called it my "management bridge." When I signed with the management company that would represent me for several years, I literally went out and crossed the bridge to "star management."

Promo photo of the author (credit: Estro Studio)

Now in this case, the catchword was quite specific and worked out relatively as planned—in an externally visible way. Not that every goal will necessarily work out exactly as imagined—but if you are sincere in the process—it is my belief, you will find "a result" from every goal you spin. Even if some goals might not become the milestones you initially anticipated, following your dreams forward becomes part of your entire life experience. Attempting your goals, you will uncover where they lead, and as you become committed to this process, your goals will refine more and more into objective successes.

One day, in the near future even, I might spin the words "champion surfer." It makes me feel "awesome" imagining I am a surfer. It gives a sense of fitness, finesse, and skill—and I really do love the beach. Maybe I would get to a beach more often and take surf lessons. Will I end up a literal champion surfer? Time will tell, but I bet I can get far enough with the idea to find satisfaction. And you never know how far you might go on any path until you investigate.

Replace non-productive thought with your catchword and upgrade your thoughts with what you desire to see yourself become. If you hear a "record" in your mind stating, "you're not good enough," remind yourself you are a "confident winner" or whatever your catchword is. Many individuals have thoughts come which are not productive, and patterns can be deeply ingrained—you do not need to judge that.

Just do your best and make the best choices you can, and this concept of "spinning" new, uplifting thoughts with your catchword, might prove very useful. It is a powerful method of dealing with unproductive thought patterns. Keep it up, keep following your steps forward and you will with time find your way—along with more belief in yourself and confidence.

Remind yourself there is "a manifestation" available of whatever you are spinning...maybe one of your goals is promotion at work. You could spin the idea of "executive." How will you feel differently? This might lead you to dress differently. Taking focus, you will find positive ideas and developments emerge as you work with creativity and continuity.

Even if an exact promotion does not actualize, you will end up a changed person. You will carry more executive qualities, which can assist you in any untold number of ways. This is part of the point; you will find a new you—even apart from any change of your obvious external reality, and you may very well find that exact opportunity you desire appearing.

Let's say you create a catchword of "compassionate human." You can repeat the thought "compassionate human, compassionate human" whenever possible on your way home. This idea can remind you and help guide your actions. Create the words you need for the times you need them! You might want to encompass "rock-star Mom," or "class-act Dad," whatever you need. Find your phrase for now and spin it in your mind.

As you keep these ideas in your mind, in various ways, you start to encompass the concepts. As this process progresses, the theory is your subconscious mind will start taking cues from you and may even assist you in ways unimagined. It takes time and repetition to convince your mind and subconscious beliefs you are serious about your goals and ideas, and that you are not just content running your life on autopilot.

Rome was not built in a day, the bigger the goal, the more time it may need to see through to fruition. This is also a fantastic method to establish a new level or new aspect to concepts already functioning in your life. You keep repeating in your mind that which you are looking to become, until it starts to feel real right now.

Miraculous events do happen, individuals win the lotto, jobs come out of seemingly nowhere. By activating inspired movement in our lives with organization, we find proactive ways to follow our FLOW. Then with our minds at ease and vitalized, from following a purpose, we pave the way for more miraculous growth or happenings. Because when we are taking constructive action, it puts a part of our thoughts at rest, as we know we are doing our best. Thus, we are not just waiting for our lives to change, but also taking an active role in the transformation.

2. Initiate mid to long-range actionable plans

In the 2nd list we discuss actual steps...and steps are important. Let us say you want a new car, you might revolve that thought in your head—someone might read your mind—and just drop it off at the front door. This could literally be possible—though it is not the usual way things work. Often, we get ideas, we organize, we create plans as best we can—and then give room for the magic of life to take shape.

The 2nd list you create highlights actual actions or steps to take, this follows up from the 1st list—or the inspirational catchword. Now, let's say your imagination has been held with the idea of "movie star" and this has turned on your excitement and imagination for life...

Start thinking of ways to follow through with this goal, pay attention to the appearance of actionable steps you might take towards this Hollywood dream. Open your mind to this step even as you are going through your daily life. Ideas may come in their own time, not only when you are sitting down to plan. Again, these are broader steps that could take even weeks or months to complete. Your daily steps will be investigated in the 3rd list.

Actionable steps could also start relatively small, in this "movie star" example, for instance, such as reading a book on acting. This is an actionable step. In this step of Law 3,

"List the Wave," the importance is you begin to take actions. You could work on fitness, take an acting class, take a yoga class...improve your diet. Keep following up on ideas that come to you. Start taking notes, prioritize what seems most important, and keep updating this list as you complete it.

Definitively, write down ideas when they emerge...having ideas notated is important for further reference. You can later check and see what thoughts have come to you. When you are able, you can organize this list of plans or actions, prioritize, and come up with a general time frame to implement them. And again, this 2nd list could be from weeks to months, though at times could even be accomplished on a shorter scale...or even into a much longer term.... Set reasonable goals or deadlines for when you hope to complete each of the tasks you set for yourself.

Be reasonable with what you can accomplish, but also be ambitious. Sometimes we can do more than we think when on a timeline. Keep incorporating these actionable ideas into your plan as long as your overriding premise or catchword still feels valid. Regarding the "movie star" scenario, maybe you will end up inspired to look at ads for local film shoots. Maybe you can start your own social media channel.

You may find after a time, that even without moving to L.A., by investigating your dream, you were able to have fun, some glamour, and maybe even a little profit. Enough to have found a sense of satisfaction. Being a "movie star," when one considers all the practicalities of the lifestyle, may not genuinely be suitable for your life. But by exploring your dream, you will have had a chance to live your life to the fullest.

And by working with the ideas and following through on plans—opportunities can snowball for you. You can never know how far you will go until you try. At some point you might find yourself at a position where your 2nd list step becomes "move to L.A.," —or maybe even Mumbai, center of the *"Bollywood"* film industry!

When we prepare ourselves and "make our luck," the world might seem to step in and take over. An influencer can discover you on your social media channel, and your career could skyrocket. Extraordinary dreams manifest every day, by exploring your goals fully, you will have honestly addressed your aspiration.

I believe by honestly addressing aspirations, we feel at ease in our lives, and release regret. This is because we have been honest with ourselves and we have engaged, and by so doing, we change. And again, surprises may greet you in the process.

3. Set a daily and weekly schedule

Moving to the 3rd list, this is your daily or weekly schedule. This is where you keep track of your short term / daily goals. My 2nd list is re-calibrated more often than the 1st list, but not as much as the 3rd list, which is basically in a constant state of flux.

An example from my life regarding this process can be taken from the writing of this book. One of my broad catchwords has been "best-selling author" or "writer," along with various permutation of that. Now, from this catchword, or 1st list, I break up my work into more actionable plans. This is the 2nd list. This list is usually time specific, but often in a longer-term way. A 2nd list example could be, "finish edits on draft by so and so date." This 2nd list may not be as exciting as the catchword, but it is practical and keeps me on task for specific plans.

Your 3rd level list will remind you of your daily requirements—to get groceries, fix the refrigerator, etc.—and for an author—book in two hours to write in the morning and afternoon, or whatever it is you need to accomplish. It keeps you on track towards your higher ambitions in a daily way. It is how to incorporate conceptual plans into actuality.

You can start small, if your catchword is, "Olympic fitness" and you have been basically sitting on a couch—besides to pick up your favorite bag of chips—scheduling 15 minutes of exercise a day is a start--and do schedule it in! By making realistic plans and completing them you will build confidence, and you might find your goals and satisfaction are achieved faster than you think.

Some individuals can get by entirely with mental lists but listing out in physical or electronic form can assist. Use something tangible. Especially as you start out, having a physical list can keep your mind and energy organized. As you get more used to the process, you can try working on a primarily mental level, but I always keep part of the listing process in physical form.

It takes creativity to organize, and it takes commitment—but it can be fun. Use your catchword to generate energy and excitement for your plans, and then see them through on the broader and daily level. Small steps are cumulative, if you can find inspiration in organizing your imagination, and keep it up day by day, you will find yourself approaching your dreams.

Finding inspiration can alter an entire procedure in life. If you are traveling on a long-anticipated trip and just cannot wait to go, packing can be an exciting adventure as you prepare for the journey—even if you normally find packing a chore. With happy anticipation, even preliminary or mundane steps can catch the joy of what is to come.

This process of organizing, along with its accompanying introspection, is hugely helpful to focus on what you want. As you refine your organization skills or personal style, feel free to tailor or expand your list making process—it is a life-long practice. Exactly how you arrange your process of identifying goals and staying on track is personal, but the 3-step process of "List the Wave" is a utilitarian way to organize, energize, and stay on track.

This concludes the 3-step practice of Law 3. The following sections of Law 3 explore applying organization, paired with proactive development, into various aspects of your life.

ORGANIZE YOUR LIFE, LIVING SPACE, AND DRESS FOR SUCCESS

A key aspect of Law 3 revolves around clear mental function. If you wonder where to begin, getting "caught up" might be the answer. It is easier to maintain your one-point focus on a specific goal if you have arranged other unresolved issues or projects.

What is it in your life you need to address? Are there long-term projects you have been meaning to complete? Or emotional issues you need to resolve? We all have aspects we tend to put off to an indefinite future time.

To achieve fresh perspective, and readiness for new projects or goals, you might consider what in your life to wrap up or accomplish. Organize and list out projects or goals that have been on your mind waiting for the right time. As you better understand what dreams you have "shelved," you can prioritize where to start. Then apply "List the Wave" and start to get "caught up!"

Recently, for me, this concept of catching up materialized in a few boxes of cassette tapes, with recordings going back even 30 years to when I was young playing the piano. There were good recordings, but the tapes were disorganized, and I wanted them better preserved and accessible. This box had stayed in the back of my mind for a long time, knowing I would one day have to "face the music" and decide on what to do.

Finally, a few days over a holiday, I dove in, found the best recordings, got them onto a flash drive and ultimately converted them into two published albums. I felt mental space open up and relief blossom as these tapes turned into a fully realized project, and it was cathartic to see the cassettes off to recycling. Completing this, I felt ready for new, fresh projects.

You might relate to this—and could even feel to be "caught up"—is insurmountable. Remember FLOW Law 1—there is always a way! This could include making the tough decisions on what is reasonable to accomplish, and even allow certain items or projects to just be scrapped or brought to recycling. However, by being impartial, identifying and listing out goals, prioritizing, and following steps, you can make it.

Physical items can be inspiring, and a multitude of personal possessions can indicate a powerful life force! However, too many unorganized items or clutter might also indicate not being emotionally "caught up" with your life or not living in the present. (This can also take place in your virtual world of computer files, pictures, etc.) It's up to you to consider your home and physical possessions, and when it is time to clean house!

If it is time to de-clutter, apply the steps of Law 3. Catchwords such as "efficient" or "organized living environment" can be your rallying cry. Work with the process for as long as it requires focus. Arranging one's living space is an on-going part of life, but sometimes requires more direct attention than others.

As you bring your physical surroundings (and virtual lives) in order, you might feel ramifications throughout your entire life. This is related to the holistic model of existence. When I feel my living-space organized and tidied up, I feel energized and ready for action—and to do whatever I want to do in that time!

As you organize, factor in items or a "staging" of your space that feels uplifting. One traditional idea is to keep pathways open for moving around and where "energy" can flow in your home. Create a sense of openness, but not too open to feel empty. Having an open, usable and yet personably inviting living space keeps my attention available for action.

Regarding items, objects can easily take on emotional representations, which can be a wonderful thing. I like to have books, art or statues, pictures, items that inspire me! And objects do not necessarily need to be expensive to be inspirational. However, if you feel swamped, or overly emotionally connected to objects, it might be time for some sorting.

In the end, it is freeing to remember, we do not need any one object for our FLOW—no matter how wonderful that one object may be. And you can always take a picture of an item and keep that! If you need help, seeking professional advice could be a way to go. Get cleaned up, organized, and free yourself to dive more freely into your FLOW!

As you sort your way through Law 3, it can be useful to have a specific location you associate with planning. It can be a desk, a spot in your house, or even an outside location—a library or favorite coffee shop! Living in Brooklyn NY, I had a favorite diner. I spent hours there over breakfast foods and coffee, reading, planning, creating, and basking in the pleasure of crossing-off lists, one after another.

View of Manhattan from Sunset Park, Brooklyn

As you upgrade your living space with clarity, how about taking a good look in the mirror?! Use Law 3 to consider your "look," and how it corresponds to your goals or catchwords. Upgrading a look, may not be that time consuming, or cost a fortune. Consider your image, you might feel a more professional image is due, or sometimes just play with your image for fun.

During intense writing or my author times, I have given myself the luxury of a few weeks of "natural" beard growth. It is not my most trimmed look, but it inspires me as someone full into his creative process. Find a look that corresponds to who you are now and what you wish to convey in your life.

I also like accessories that feel sharp or motivational. I have a pair of cufflinks with the image of the god Mercury on them, which I bought before singing at a celebrity-laden concert in NYC. These items themselves, along with the associated time and place of purchase, always lift me up when I see them, and the same goes for a few rings I have. Remember, items need not be name brand or expensive, but items that fit to you with a consistent psychological impact can be inspiring.

My mentor, the major twentieth-century opera star Shirley Verrett, always paid attention to clothing and fashion. She would remind us the importance of our look for meetings, auditions, and of course, onstage in concerts. And she was known to say, "always remember the shoes—especially on stage!" Let's follow Shirley Verrett's advice, pay attention to your fashion and details, shoes included!

ORGANIZE YOUR FINANCIAL MIND

Keeping track of finances and financial goals is an on-going process. Clarity around your finances, as well as directly facing your financial achievements and challenges is an integral part of being comfortable, confident, and ready to get on with your life.

Investing time in increasing your financial education and financial opportunities can be made into a great "catchword." This could be learning about basic and more advanced saving and investment possibilities, and even dealing directly with whatever financial challenges you might need to organize and structure for your situation.

Being upfront with yourself and others is often the best method. You will most likely have more opportunities to work through your situations, and have others more willing to assist you, when you are. Often there are more opportunities available to us upon investigation than we might have first considered.

For me, part of what that meant after I relocated to NYC was to get a real estate license to better understand the market there. After a few years, being settled in my primary career, I even realized the opportunity for real estate transactions.

This step of furthering your financial understanding is up to you, it is up to your time and the extent of your dreams. However, as money is a form of energy, it is empowering to understand your basic financial choices and opportunities.

ORGANIZE INTO CREATIVITY

As you keep spinning positively inspired thoughts, catchwords, and take proactive actions, it is also important to find time to "let go" and give room for your impulses and actions to play themselves out. If you have been busy spinning your world, it might be time to let the "tea leaves settle" and allow the *chi* to sink. We need time to rest our minds and bodies and find states of receptivity to invite in creativity. Letting the mind and thoughts alone, can also be an equally productive state.

The creative process includes navigating emotional and physical balance. There is a reoccurring idea in this book of using a creative process to discover and take action, see what happens, and then follow up with corresponding actions. The FLOW Laws themselves came to me in a creative way, that felt deeper than my conscious mind. Though we may not be able to consciously determine when creative ideas will hit, we can create an environment in our lives and minds that stays open to creativity.

Individuals throughout history have used methods of quieting the mind in preparation for creative states, as ways to deeply rest and refresh, prepare for upcoming action, and for many other positive ramifications. Meditation may be as simple as finding a few moments to appreciate nature, or just to appreciate a moment. There are many forms of meditation. Using the 1st step catchword is itself a kind of meditation or mantra.

Even our daily rituals can serve as meditations—or moving meditations—that bring comfort and focus. We wake up, brew coffee, read the newspaper, take out the dog, or whatever it is we do to start our mornings. Ritual as a concept has been long used in innumerable ways by cultures to bring positive states where creativity can be tapped, and more productivity achieved. Do you have rituals or practices that make you more available to higher, deeper, or more pleasant and creative thoughts or states?

Rituals can even be as straightforward as setting certain structures to a daily regime, setting a consistent wake-up time, or taking a daily walk in the park. Organizing your time is not only about proactive moments but also the introspective and reflective. Lighting a candle or flame has been a long practice in humanity and holds a vast repository of symbolic imagery.

For the followers of Zoroaster, which is considered one of the earliest—if not the earliest—of *revealed* religions, the flame was considered a highest representation of creative energy or God. Throughout history, individuals have found success in, or attributed success to, their faith in a higher power or powers. This could be in God or gods, in Life itself, or even trust in one's higher self to work out life in an all-around best way.

Along with the principle of ritual, there is the contrasting aspect of attempting something new, even a minor adjustment in the route home, for instance. Incorporating ways to new perspective might even be considered a ritual of its own! The trip discussed at the book's beginning, was intended to be a life experience, and life changing. Visiting a location with a special quality, be it some extraordinary natural feature such as by the ocean—whatever draws a person—can have a profound effect on our emotional and physical states. A well-conceived break from life, even a short vacation, can in a very real sense reset our lives.

Of course, art and music are other powerful forces for uplifting and bringing individuals to heightened or even altered states of consciousness. Find methods to revive and refresh yourself. It could be as simple as hydrotherapy in a bath, it's whatever floats your boat! By incorporating small moments in our lives, we can increase our sense of wellbeing and enjoyment of life, and ultimately our productivity, one step at a time.

SEE WHERE THE FLOW LEADS

As you keep on following these points, see where your experiences lead. Also notice what begins to interest you. You may continue with dreams or your dreams might modify to new ones along the way.

Stay creative, flexible and get to the core of what you want. If one of your dreams has been sports car ownership and it is not happening, consider the dream deeply. Is this manifestation truly for you? Or would you honestly be happier to take the bus and save the effort. You can always rent the car of your dreams for a weekend and enjoy it—saving yourself financing, washing it, and daily parking!

You can make huge strides organizing your dreams right now. This process is fun, can be fast, and has little to no associated cost. As you organize and follow the 3-step plan presented in "List the Wave" you will gain confidence in directing your life. And as you see yourself organizing the various aspects of your life, you will feel better and better that your greater dreams have more space to be revealed.

MEDITATION

As I walk my path of life, I am at ease and confident in my understanding of how to organize, follow, and simultaneously create my dreams. All the while I am trusting in the co-creative nature of the world, and I will accept all good opportunities that arise.

FLOW Law 4

"Time the Wave"

> Encounter in Cambodia—a foreign agent?!
> Make the pancakes while the griddle is hot
> Enjoy the FLOW and get things done simultaneously
> Make friends with time / the sky, the planets, and stars
> Make the move when the spirit calls
> Silence and to "Time the Wave"
> Meditation

    As our lives move along incorporating the FLOW system, we create opportunities, and we also find opportunities appearing. I think of these opportunities as windows, almost as tangible things, I imagine as if they exist in a reality of their own—energetic window opportunities. Preparing ourselves in inspired ways, new opportunities seem to have more frequency of appearing. At first glimmer of window of opportunity's opening, it is vital to peer in and see what is coming while the magic is fresh.

    One can question how these opportunities develop... From previous work on the part of the individuals in the creative state? From chance, good luck?... Sometimes events can almost feel predestined. It does not really matter how opportunity appears, but in the actualization of the opportunity, in the making use of possibilities.

"Time the Wave" is another aspect of the FLOW system. This is the momentary aspect, or the timing aspect of the system—the *when* in "Catch the Wave." It is the principle that the FLOW comes in a specific time or timing. It is another functioning of life and represents our continuous living in the moment.

Wherever we find ourselves we can attempt equanimity, trusting into wellbeing and possibility. Although this is true, and perhaps more than we can fathom, there are some opportunities on Earth which we call time sensitive.

Let's say one arrives on earth, and as a child maturing, the overwhelming dream for this young human is to become a child actor. Fast forward a few years, the child is now getting on 14 years old, the "child actor dream" now needs modification. There is such a thing as a window of opportunity, though the good news is that the child can still follow the dream of a teen actor.

Basically, we want to enjoy our dreams sooner than later. If we have been assembling our dreams, and opportunities arise, it is in our best interest and most pleasure to go with the course, in the now. Of course, we can reassemble dreams and potential can be limitless—if we have flexibility as an aspect of the deal—but why wait? Let's start up right now!

And how to start?!

First, dare to take opportunities as they arise, even small ones. Feel more open to jump in with options that feel positive and new, especially if the opportunities correspond to your dreams. Along with this, keep on developing heightened discernment as to your use of time.

For achievement one often needs right actions to bring motion to life. I appreciate taking actions when they feel inspired and in a direction to which I am committed. In Law 2 we began developing excitement in a general way and then focused it during Law 3. Now as you consider the principle of time, you consider the arrangement of effort in regard to taking actions, as well as developing discernment in which opportunities to take.

As you have worked with your catchword in Law 3, and have found ideas for movement in your life, where is it leading? What opportunities are you uncovering and how do they interest you? Are there ideas that are fulfilling, have you found anything exciting?

What opportunities seem to be arising as if on their own? Are there any? Think of your dreams, what is arising, and then think of the practicalities. Can options that arise be managed within the framework of the current financial status or can you find alternative methods to manage the dreams?

If you find an opportunity developing, and it corresponds to a current "catch word,"—or might be developing a new one—as discussed in FLOW Law 3, you might want to go with it. Higher functioning people will also have ability to handle more opportunities at once—and / or can delegate to someone else. Though still there are limits to options anyone can follow through at one point.

Pay attention to signs you are receiving, and those signs can happen at any moment. Notice when you feel a tug of the spirit—which you might think of as a combination of mental and / or emotional engagement or excitement. And pointedly, what do you feel is the right step for now? Some moments are for planning, or enjoying the fruits of our labor, and then arrives a time for action.

Along with your internal thoughts and intuition, messages might appear from seemingly outside sources of inspiration.

Various happenings could trigger seemingly unrelated thoughts or ideas, as well as opportunities may directly appear for the taking. Pay attention to the voice of others, individuals advising you to "go ahead" or even "proceed with caution" with certain projects. These might be important indicators for you. When everything is lining-up for "go ahead" and "this is the time" it might be the chance to advance.

As more and more opportunities come to you, you will need added discernment. Do some due diligence. Does the initial idea still hold water but need modification? Is there value enough in a project considering its time cost? Is this an opportunity to fulfill one of your broad level goals? Is there enough chance for success to merit the opportunity? There is always a merit / risk ratio. After analysis, determine if it is worth jumping in. The more you hone your senses, the faster the process becomes.

Now, as mentioned, I love travel. My level of enjoyment in moving around on the planet is in a rare percentile. I thrive to see the world and experience different cultures and meet new people. Even the Earth's topography and how the local environments in their permutations all around the globe affected local cultural development is extremely fascinating to me. This desire was advantageous for a career as a singer, that took me traveling as much as it did. Along with career related business, I have also embarked on many personal adventures taking me around the globe. During one of the trips, I found myself presented with an unforeseen set of events...

ENCOUNTER IN CAMBODIA— A FOREIGN AGENT?!

On one flight into Cambodia, an exceedingly kind older Austrian man was two seats away from me, with no one seated in between. He had questions for the flight attendant but only speaking German, he did not receive answers that satisfied. Having lived in Germany and speaking a relatively fluent German, I started conversing with him. He seldom traveled, but for many years had been filled with a desire to see the ruins of Angkor Wat and thus embarked upon this travel. I clarified his inquiry regarding the landing card and any other questions he had, and then I heard from the seat in front of me...

"*Sie sprechen ein sehr schoenes Deutsch.*" ("You speak a very lovely German.")

Turning while rising from the row in front of me ascended a strikingly beautiful woman. I quickly discovered—at that point with no great surprise—she hailed from Germany, in particular that area of Germany that had been the former East. Tall, with straightened dark hair, she possessed a pair of dark, intelligent—you might say captivating—eyes. We chatted about my time in Germany—using a mix of German and English—and after landing continued as we descended the stair into the sunlight of a bright Cambodian afternoon.

As we deplaned, she realized she was without cash, either in the local currency or US dollars. Shortly we would require cash for a small fee for the travel visa, taxi to the hotel, plus any other miscellaneous necessities. I wished to assist her and offered to loan the equivalent of 30 or 40 US dollars. Politely refusing, we attempted to locate an ATM briefly as we entered the airport. However, as no option was found, she quickly accepted the assistance.

Reconvening after securing our travel visas, she declared, "Let's meet in the city to return the cash in a few days' time... But where?" An idea flashed in my mind, *The Red Piano* lounge of *Tomb Raider Cocktail* fame. (This drink was created for Angelina Jolie during her time in Cambodia shooting the film of the same name.) Only vaguely familiar with local venues, I had glanced an ad for this touristic spot, and it had suddenly appeared in my mind as the most alluring option.

After parting, on way to the hotel, I considered her and her sharp and classy impression. She seemed so put together... Perhaps too put together? And so self-composed, why was she without dollars or otherwise any currency on the plane? A recollection of an old spy film emerged in my thoughts, so much so, I questioned for a minute, "Was she who she claimed to be?" Or had I been thoroughly played, rather convincingly, for a mere 35 USD?! Albeit stunning—could I even ascertain if she were truly German after all?! And what about our upcoming meeting? Would she show?...

"Had I conversed with an international agent?!"

The agent or spy scenario—inspired by my black and white film recollections—pleased and amused me. Not genuinely believing her a spy, it did add an atmospheric effect, perfectly complementing our backdrop in this relatively remote Southeast Asian region surrounded by the archeological wonders of an ancient civilization. I adored the poetry of it, and to be shortly meeting her at *The Red Piano*... Wheresoever better to meet a foreign intelligence correspondent than *The Red Piano*! It resounded perfectly, a resplendent "film noir."

In the following days, as I explored ancient jungle ruins with a friend, the upcoming meeting faded into the backdrop of tuk-tuk rides and hikes through exotic flora and miraculous monuments. Then as the day for the meeting arrived, I admit to the excitement. Would she show up? Would we be able to find each other at the location?!

That evening, sitting at one of the low tables in *The Red Piano*, I was beyond delighted when she appeared at the entrance, her entire person still sparkling. I greeted her at the door and escorting her to the table we began to catch up on the last few days of our adventures and our time traveling in Asia in general. It was another magical moment.

She showed genuine interest in my life—especially in how I had all these interesting experiences around the world about which we had been conversing. She inquired how I envisioned a life philosophy or made my approach to reality. And then she directly asked me, "Can you recommend a book? A book that will tie all this together?"

I replied, "I enjoy a great number of books around the subject, however, exactly what I am speaking about now, well maybe no... Maybe I need to write one!"

> She smiled, nodded her head, perhaps a wink, and kept sparkling...was that a dare?

Angor Wat, Cambodia

Her current location or language of choice is a mystery. She might have truly been an agent, but perhaps an agent of a different sort. She gave me encouragement for a book which had not yet been born. The window of opportunity to write this book had not yet appeared, yet she served as an agent of the World (or an agent of the FLOW Freedom Laws of the World ™!) to plant a seed for this book, one day to come to fruition.

That time in Cambodia was already several years ago. In this book's *Prescript*, upon mentioning the book's idea appeared at once, that was to indicate this present form of the FLOW Freedom Laws of the World. ™ It does not discount the point that ideas had been forming and fermenting for some time. Even during the time in Cambodia, I received hints from the World, such as from this "FLOW agent."

Your life experiences can be leading towards any number of goals. It requires time to reveal how developments unfold. On the one hand, we want to be actively forming plans, and this is making use of time. However, simultaneously, once the time is ripe, movement and ideas can come fast—even feeling all at once. If it is taking some time to fulfill your dreams, give yourself a break. Just keep doing your best and allow the unfolding in time.

Moments of grand inspiration may not be easily timed but following your FLOW, you can prepare as you go, more than you consciously understand. And when inspiration does appear, and might even hit like lightning, then it is crucial to take the hint and go with it.

As the FLOW Laws landed in my mind, walking out of the shopping mall, they came quickly. It was in a simplistic version, but there appeared a basic line-up of the FLOW Laws, the basis for the introduction and flashes of interrelating stories. The book came as if revealed. Thus, though large-scale projects may be cumulations of thoughts and insights gathered over time, the form can come suddenly. When the FLOW hit, I was convinced of the book, of its importance, and its validity. But it still required uncountable hours of time to write, revise, and satisfactorily have it down on the page.

MAKE THE PANCAKES WHILE THE GRIDDLE IS HOT

After receiving the epiphany to write this book, at the shopping mall in Busan, South Korea, I was extremely enthusiastic. However, the next morning, upon waking, the sky was dark with clouds and was heavily raining. It was hard to think of the day as other than gloomy. The memory of the previous day's excitement regarding the book had waned, though the ideas were still present, still on my mind. I thought, "I need to give this a try, just see what comes down on paper if I start. Will the magic of yesterday continue once I give this a chance?"

I reminded myself of the excitement, how much I had loved the idea, and to trust in the concept, to trust in the FLOW. Start and see what happens, start writing and see if anything emerges. Once I sat down in the coffee shop with a cup of coffee and my computer, the memories of the previous day started coming back to flood me and I wrote for a few hours without stop. I had captured the initial stories, the book's framework, and the FLOW Laws all in one session.

Was it fun, was it passionate, was it in a FLOW that felt bigger than myself? You bet. But it did take effort! Certainly. And I was tired out after that writing spree, but still, it was a labor of fun. In that state of enjoyment, I try to get my projects completed. A state of positive movement, and not from obligation or requirement.

I believe in this case, at least in part, things worked because I was able to get started when the window of time was right, when the inspiration was fresh, and I was able to ride that. Had I missed that moment; this book might not have been. And of course, the book did take a lot more consistency, effort, and time drafting afterwards; however, by hitting the window of time, the project was born.

ENJOY THE FLOW AND GET THINGS DONE SIMULTANEOUSLY

As you continue your FLOW path, working more and more seamlessly in time, sometimes you can accomplish goals simultaneously, even when you did not expect it. An example from my life relates to one of my interests since I was a young man, the work of psychologist / philosopher Carl Jung.

I had been interested in his writings and his great impact on culture and Western psychology—especially how he brought into the field of psychology ancient ideas and the idea of archetypes. And I have spent a good amount of time reading through his memoirs and other writings and I remember him genuinely appreciating the idea and concept of time.

This specific "Time the Wave" multitasking opportunity came on an audition tour throughout the German speaking world, primarily Germany and Austria, embarked on before moving to NYC. Many wonderful opera houses grace these areas, and I wanted to explore opportunities. While on the tour, I initiated important networking with managers and professionals, as well as learned a great deal about the European system. And of course, there was the pleasure of viewing fantastic opera productions and concerts; including times sitting in on rehearsals and going backstage to see the system, up-close and firsthand.

While staying with a friend in North West Germany near Cologne, this fascinating chance emerged. Dwelling in the German countryside, in a voluminous house refurbished and rebuilt incorporating ancient structures—including a part of an old barn—was a special and picturesque time. This friend, a philosophical and intuitive woman, held insightful conversations and at one point we came to speak of the work of Carl Jung. During the conversation, she mentioned to me, "Actually, I know one of his nieces!"

I was surprised and delighted for the revelation, as Carl Jung is iconic to me—in fact, to most every student of western Psychology I might insert! Upon hearing my interest, she stated she would call and introduce me to the niece.

It was one of those rare chances and moments in time. I had no idea exploring the personal world of Carl Jung would avail itself while on this trip. I certainly jumped at the opportunity.

My friend made the phone call, and the "niece" and I spoke on the phone—she wanted to hear my voice before she would meet in person—and we eventually met when I arrived in Munich in the train station. And as she occasionally rented out one of her rooms for short term lodging, I ended up two weeks at her residence in Munich later that month. What a prospect to have such a historic connection while simultaneously singing auditions in southern Germany!

Time spent with her was even more special than anticipated. Besides her insights into Carl Jung, she herself was a very charismatic and highly developed individual. And to be entirely clear with her relation, it turns out she was not technically a niece of Jung, her father was I believe Carl Jung's cousin. Still it was a close relation, and she was part of the family. She had spent time with Carl Jung on numerous occasions as a young girl and she had always addressed him as "Uncle Carl."

I heard many stories of Uncle Carl on that trip, even Jung family reminiscences and ideals she felt had been in the family consciousness for generations. I became an insider into a history I was so curious about. This time in Munich with the niece was exceptional and is a time I still cherish.

Before I left, we decided to have a pair of *Abschied* (parting) events. I brought her to a concert of *Winterreise* (Winter's journey), a song cycle of Schubert, sung by the famous bass-baritone Thomas Quasthoff. It was a fairy tale evening winding our way thru ancient paths and majestic promenades thru the city of Munich to that exceptional concert.

For her part, she brought me along to the Oktoberfest in Munich. It was a personal yearly-ritual for her, and for that year, I accompanied her. And perhaps not surprisingly, this, one of our final moments on that adventure together, relates deeply to the idea of time. She showed a sage sense of poetry in the honoring of time.

Every year at the Munich Oktoberfest there is a great Ferris wheel, and this wheel stood alike to a giant representation of a Wheel of Time. She rode this giant Ferris wheel in the Oktoberfest each year, and that year, we together sat across the swaying cabin from each other. As the car gently swung, spinning us up and down around this giant wheel, we became silent. We rotated up and down and the wheel turned and turned; and we silently gazed out on the festival, into the trees and the city of Munich.

A few moments as we were perched high atop the wheel, I stole a glance at her. She was silent and contemplative. She seemed in those moments, eternal and incredibly wise. We were both sorry that I was leaving—but what a memory and occasion to have had—and the wheel kept on spinning. Indeed, like the great Wheel of Time.

When one is moving "in time," or when one is in a state of "Time the Wave," one might not even realize being on this cusp of time. So in sync with the giant wheel, so in the FLOW, it is as if there is no friction holding you back and you may not realize how smoothly and quickly you progress. As you merge with your FLOW, adapting the various FLOW Laws into your life, you will be working with time in a higher and higher way. In your enjoyment and fulfillment, you may not even realize your situation, because in the FLOW, one may not even notice the current.

Temple in the tundra, Inner Mongolia, China

MAKE FRIENDS WITH TIME / TIME IN THE SKY, THE PLANETS, AND STARS

My overarching mindset regarding *time*, an idea I came up with years ago, is one to keep. It might seem a little unusual, but it is the idea to "make friends" with time.

When you develop a relationship and love of time, time will love you back.

This thought I truly cherish. It is an overriding principle worth remembering. A relationship is not something which happens once and is done, it is on-going, and that is a way I relate to the idea of time. Time is a daily experience but also a mysterious phenomenon. It seems commonplace, but in the world of physics, it is a whole complex of study, and ramifications can be mind-blowing.

This idea of creating a relationship with time is also not new. Many ancient cultures had a god or goddess of time, and time became personified. One could develop more directly a relationship with time through the specific deity, one could in essence directly worship time. In Greece there was Chronos, who was in control of time or the personification of time, thus, the term "chronology." And in India, there is still worshiped the god, Kalabairava, encompassing and being the Lord of Time.

Now there are many ways to work on practical time management—and using lists as in Law 3 is one. You can personally consider ways to organize and make more efficient use of your time. But even beyond the specifics of your time management, create a desire to do your best with your time as a life principle. This desire to be more "in touch" with time is a beautiful idea. And remember, these FLOW Laws, starting from the first one, "Catch the Wave," are about your time moving forward, not concerned over previous or past opportunity.

A ground state of *loving time* is a framework from which all the other time management techniques can spring. Find ways to make time and time management feel powerful to you. When I realized my name *Temporelli* can be broken up into the root word of *tempo* (time) and a name ending *–elli* (this ending is ubiquitous in Northern Italy surnames) I was excited. It gave me a chance to feel personal about the concept of time.

The author on boat, Lake Atitlan, Guatemala

Time is celestial. We measure time by how long our planet revolves around the sun. There are vast, poetic, and generally fascinating ideas around the concept of time and its relation to our lives. Ancient cultures maintained curious and manifold thoughts on time—and these cultures had specific assessments regarding celestial movements and time that would be related now to astronomy and astrology.

Traditional cultures would plant, harvest, and plan their lives in general around the movement of the moon, the planets, and the stars. I even remember as a young boy, the older generation of Italian friends relating to me stories how the planting, trimming and harvest of the grapes would be set around the phases of the moon, back in the old country.

Before the Mayan calendar was said to come to a cyclic end in 2012, I had a chance to study with Mayan shamans in Guatemala. In those meetings and discussions, we talked about the nature of time held by ancient peoples and the concept of ages, large-scale time frames, periods, or époques. Interesting aspects I encountered also included diagrams drawn of the Mayan spiraling of time. And this fascination with time and related concepts was widespread in the ancient world, it was not unique with the Mayans.

Early cultures had an idea that human action or timing could be—or should be—associated with the movement of celestial bodies in the sky. In India there is the Vedic tradition relating to the concept of time, with timing relations happening on various levels. Vedic thought assumes certain influences occur during the various hours of the day, the days of the week, the year—even the various years of a person's life.

As one goes through life, it is felt in the Vedic world—and other similar world views—that stages are influenced by differing forces, and these differing stages will have various impacts. These forces can relate to the planets, the stars, among other forces, and it is in one's best interest to work with the time and forces at hand in the most beneficial ways possible. Many groups, including the Mayans, and Western astrology, had related ideas explicit or implicit in the cultures.

Whether you are curious or dubious of the ideas of astrological influences, I think we all have had times when it feels easier to move ahead, and times when life feels more of a challenge. For most productivity, sometimes we keep going no matter what—that is "sticking with it." However, timing is vital, and for whatever reasons, sometimes we need to alter our focus. Find what you feel is the best use of your time, at the moment. If some aspect does not feel in the right timing, do something else. Consider your options with your time and realize, sometimes we even need to give ourselves a rest. It can also be encouraging to remember that "times will change."

It is important to find the right timing for activities, and this can be influenced by personal circumstance, or even the general state of the world. Shoveling snow and sunbathing are great activities, but often seasonal. Keep balancing your management of time, and figure out timings, or find systems or ideas that work for you.

In general, feel inspired to go out and make use of time. Trust the right time for action, and then the time for rest, and acceptance at other times. And keep being kind and compassionate with yourself; as you follow the FLOW Law system, sooner or later, you will find things working out for you with more consistency.

MAKE THE MOVE WHEN THE SPIRIT CALLS

As you focus on developing your sense of how to use time, you want to pay attention to your intuition around using time. You want to sharpen your "gut instincts" on direction and planning. Just having this idea in your mind helps.

You begin to see more opportunities and feel that "tug of the spirit"—and moments or "clues" can come anywhere and anytime. Some people will say when you start opening your mind's eye to the possibilities around you, it is not that more opportunities arise, it is just that you make more use of them. I like to think that in an interesting quantum quirk of the way things work, you actually do start attracting more opportunities and more like-minded people around you, as you sharpen your awareness.

What truly matters is, getting into your FLOW, opportunities appear. After several years of master's and doctoral study in Ann Arbor, Michigan, I felt a noteworthy tug of the spirit, and it changed the direction of my life. This was in a time when I had lived comfortably in the same apartment for the duration of graduate study; I was accustomed to my life and felt content.

Moving forward with life, I considered where to go and what to do. I played with ideas of moving to different cities, but when it came down to it, I cherished my apartment, comfortable life and nearby family and friends. However, shortly after I had signed the apartment lease for another year, I happened to encounter one of my professors at the university—and his reaction, in a way, equaled what I had been taught up to then.

Upon this chance meeting, he asked my upcoming plans. I happily replied I would stay right where I was, at least for the next year. He leapt out of his skin, "Get out of here, nothing will happen for you here. Go to New York City, now. Fly. Now!"

I was shocked. And in that moment, my life changed.

Quickly, I sublet my then current apartment, literally packed the van, and a few weeks later drove into NYC. That moment became a monumental message for me and a window of opportunity I could not ignore. I leapt in while the option was open.

Another window of opportunity, to interact with individuals I would never otherwise have a chance to meet, is on an airplane, or in travel in general. Maybe it is that people are excited to travel or the atmosphere is thinner up in the air. I have gained insights and travel companionships simply by approaching fellow travelers waiting with me in lounges or sitting on a plane or train—of course, only if the interest is mutual. On a plane I was even once seated next to a TV producer, whose work I had been a long-time fan of, and we ended up becoming great friends.

A few years after my time in Guatemala, I was on a flight landing in NYC and then transiting onwards. Our flight ended up delayed for several hours, which understandably did not please many of the passengers. However, there was a charismatic man seated next to me who had lived in Belize, Central America...

He encouraged me to visit that country as well. He charmed me with stories of the towns and villages, the ocean, and the people of the country. I told him I loved seeing jungle and he said the jungle was so rich, "If you spit a lime seed, it will start growing into a tree in a week." At least in part, thanks to meeting him, after that chance meeting on a layover, I have had many wonderful adventures in Belize.

Recently, again in a NYC airport, I found myself in a lengthy security line. It had seemed long, but as the line turned a corner...then I really saw how long of a line it truly was. I thought to myself, "There has just got to be something more for me in this moment."

I looked around and the person next to me drew my attention. I started speaking with him and it turned out he is a best-selling author. We conversed about his best-seller book, about writing, and about the publishing process in general. Despite my initial concern about the lengthy line, by the time we made it through security, I was even almost disappointed to end the discussion!

Sky above La Grande-Motte, French Alps

SILENCE AND TO "TIME THE WAVE"

Discernment is knowing when to act and when to refrain from action. This includes appreciating the beauty of boundaries between actions. It is taking moments to feel silence and stillness, to enjoy the time between the notes.

In becoming a musician, one learns this concept that "silence speaks." As a novice, most important seems getting all the notes, that is pushing down the keys—and sometimes just as fast as you can. However, as you develop, placing the notes in time, and paying attention to the space around the notes, also takes precedent. In painting or art, this can be referred to as negative space—the space around an object of interest.

It is the same in life, knowing when to work hard and then when to throw in the towel. Time for rest and recovery can be as important as the work itself. And though it is possible to achieve states requiring less sleep, we humans still need time to recharge, time for rest, time for sleep and rejuvenation, time to indulge in non-activity.

In my early days in NYC, if I was not on an engagement, I often felt I was missing out. I wanted my main dream to happen at once, as fast as possible. This was positive in its ambition, but it is also important to enjoy and regroup.

Now if there is a little more time off, if there is a chance to take a walk in the park, I can appreciate it more for what it is and not think that I should be out doing something "productive." This perhaps comes naturally as one sees dreams coming to fruition, but it also is a result of a new understanding of the FLOW Laws of life. And remember the power of small efforts that build up over time. Even if day-by-day activity seems inconsequential, such as laying one piece of paper on another, in due course there will be a huge stack.

Keep on with "Time the Wave," fulfill the moment, jump into the *wave* of what you wish—and then learn to discern timing and the core of your desires. Keep it light, though the waves FLOW up and down. I gave myself time before writing this book…it took some years between Cambodia and the moment of revelation…I let the right moment in time appear in its due course. By catching the cusp of time, you will stay the course to *meaning* and set up a future more satisfying, exciting, and joyful than you ever imagined.

MEDITATION

I ready myself for windows of opportunity and positivity. I understand that various periods of life have unique characteristics, and I cherish them all. Through appreciation—even if the current of life seems slow—I trust into the FLOW of the greater timing.

FLOW Law 5

"Zen the Wave"

> Daily steps, daily Zen
> Generosity
> Universal Zen—it will work for you
> Zen it big
> Beyond your "self" and into your transcendence
> Meditation

Starting out in New York City, I remember speaking with an established singing "guru" about a certain opera conductor. This conductor had assisted several singers to advance their careers. I made a comment about the power of the conductor's influence and this guru said, "But don't you think it's we ourselves who either make or break our career?"

In Law 5, we investigate the angle that it is ultimately we ourselves who create our future. We look at our idea of "self" and how our personal vision may or may not be assisting us in our development. Often, there is a path readily available for development—perhaps quicker than imagined. The success, or a success you might desire, can be right around the corner.

Perhaps surprisingly, issues may at times not be with others or with the system. Sometimes the issue is with our own selves blocking our progress. In "Zen the Wave," you make sure that you are not the one getting in your own way. As the FLOW brings you to your goals, keep your mind and focus on the things you want, keep focus on the essential.

When personal issues draw attention, and intentions away from that which we genuinely want, that is when to "Zen the Wave." It is to move our focus back to that which is most productive for our goals. "Zen the Wave" is streamlining our lives and intentions. To be successful, we need focus and attention on the essentials. We remove the clutter of non-essentials from our mind in "Zen the Wave." It is a question of priorities, and we do that which need be done, even if remedial.

This also requires security in our sense of *self*, enough that we do not let personal slights or differences divert us from our goals. By maintaining a vantage of higher motivations and instincts, while mitigating small-minded thoughts or inclinations, we come quicker into the lives we most want.

In "Zen the Wave" you "Zen," or release, that which is holding you back. Stay focused on that which you want, dropping unnecessary actions, thoughts or aspects of "self" that are non-productive. You do, however, follow necessary steps and think big. As you let personal issues out of the way, and trust in the universality of these Laws, you will find your FLOW.

DAILY STEPS, DAILY ZEN

As we discuss this "Zen the Wave" concept further, we will consider ideas of self-development and personality, the idea of the "self" or the "ego," and how to address it in the FLOW system. In this book I refer to various philosophical paths and practices, and if one explores different systems, one may hear ideas such as "transcending the ego," which often rings of spiritual experience, even to a cosmic or monumental way.

Dong Baek Island, Busan, South Korea

My interest in various philosophies and methodologies lead me to having "sat" in meditation with numerous Zen masters, Western and Eastern, including a monastic abbot in Japan. Studying a system based upon Korean Buddhism for a few years, weekly I would spend time settled cross-legged on cushions, learning from a Korean mountain-temple trained teacher principles of seated meditation and classic Korean Buddhism.

Hearing the term "Zen the Wave," thoughts and associations might include sublime transcendence of the self and merging with all that is, at least in a conceptual form. And that is a beautiful image, having a personal experience of transcendence, or especially learning a practice to employ for peace and well-being, can be wonderful. But in the FLOW system, the primary aspect we focus on regarding the "self," is a prioritization of goals, and mitigation of aspects of yourself which keep you from your success.

Once, when I was singing a benefit concert on one of the Caribbean Islands, we were hosted by a remarkably successful and accomplished person. He impressed me with his charm and demeanor. He had worked in high-level banking and had been acquainted with some of the most wealthy and influential individuals, especially of Central and South America.

We hit it off together and had ample time to chat and meet on a more personal level. We had a marvelous time driving around the island to attend various functions, luncheons, dinners, and events—as a side note, I also met many top-chefs on the island with him and we enjoyed many excellent culinary experiences! And he even taught me to drive a manual transmission! ...to a relative amount of success...one afternoon as we toured around the island.

During the course of events, he shared his philosophy of life—it was an exceptional opportunity. Discussing his life approach, including aspects of relating to others in a successful way, he said, "If you want to be successful, you cannot have an *ego*."

This was said with import—and it rang in my mind. I could feel it was vital to grasp, and he meant it in a practical way. He did not speak of *ego* in the sense of spiritual transcendence. He implied, we need to work with others, and often need to pull our own agendas and personal feelings out of the way. That is a way to get the job done, and at key moments, this considerably basic idea can make all the difference in a career and life.

If you sit down at a business meeting and a client shows support for a political ideology that is the cardinal opposite of your own belief system, you might want to let that go if it is not relating to the deal at hand. One needs flexibility to release personal feelings and focus on that which is more important. If we wish to be successful in life, we need to work with others. And the more in your FLOW in general, the more you will be able to relate to various types of people.

Even with this ideal of "no ego," you can still have high self-esteem. You can, and often should, think highly of yourself, these ideas are not mutually exclusive. We should think highly—and honesty—about ourselves. By thinking well of yourself—in a realistic way—you can accomplish what you want.

Of course, over-confidence or being unrealistic regarding ability can get out of hand. However, to shoot far, sometimes it requires saying "Yes," even if you are currently not quite ready, but can learn and figure out the details as you go. Generally, a good self-esteem is a beneficial thing. As you "Zen the Wave" you may even more clearly see the core or extent of your true abilities, and perhaps even feel better about yourself.

"Zen out" from your life that which is holding you back, personality, preferences, or attitudes which might not allow you to take opportunities available for your benefit. This form of ego takes you off your path to an unnecessary tangent. It is the ego which feels you would rather "teach someone a lesson" than get along with your own life. It is the thought, "Even if it cost me progressing in my best direction, I will not let that person get ahead." Do what you want to for yourself, without wasting time or energy on retaliation for no good reason—possibly you were even a part of an initial issue. Do not swerve from your path to prove an unnecessary point.

"Zen the Wave" teaches us to be adaptive and appreciate new vision. "Zen the Wave" relates to the "Zen of the sideways glance," in that certain irrelevant realities at times need be ignored, to focus on a goal. However, there may be aspects of your life you should face directly. If a task at hand requires attention, focus laser-like attention and deal with what needs to be done, blustering aspects of personality aside. That is to "Zen the Wave."

"Zen the Wave" is staying open to learn. Your FLOW will guide you to higher understanding and awareness, but only if you allow yourself to see or access it. When you trust your momentum, you can release a sense of pressure to account for the unaccountable or unknowable. You can relax more, with faith and trust in the process.

This can bring profound change if you follow these premises, and older thoughts or ideas may no longer be useful. You may find a new path emerge, or you may find more ease and joy in your life as it is. As you "Zen the Wave" you might even find yourself emerging as a new person. You, just better! Like the phoenix rising from its own ashes.

Be willing to take the steps needed, we all need to take steps to our development. If the world is offering opportunities for growth, be willing to put in the effort. It is good to want advancement *now*, but be willing to take the steps necessary to advancement. Attempting to completely jump steps, whether personal or professional, can at times lead to issues down the line. Moving fast is desirable, but one can learn a lot from a journey. When a monk first would join the temple, often initial training would be to sweep out the courtyard.

Be even willing, if you can deem it useful, to do jobs or projects you feel are below your skillset or capacity, especially if these actions can help your team or superiors. This may allow you more options down the road. As in all the FLOW Laws, look for the balance and appreciate your place of being right now. Now is a great place to be.

GENEROSITY

Getting into an emotional place of thankfulness for your life and gratitude for just being alive is indeed a great attitude to have. In this state, you are more open to the actions which will bring you to your success. But what if you still cannot get the idea out of your head that things have not gone well for you and that you deserve more? That the world owes you...

Perhaps that is the case, and more is already on the way. The thing is we all have felt underappreciated or undervalued. It has been said in the music business, if you do ten auditions and receive one engagement offer from them, those are good odds. That is all well and good in theory—but landing one job out of ten might not initially feel like success.

Not every opportunity pans out. However, looking back on my life, if I did not receive one opportunity—and even if I were disappointed about it—something else would inevitably be available to do. If one specific circumstance did not turn out, there was something to pay attention to or accomplish in its place.

Once as I was musing on the idea of desire for "more" or growth, I had a thought. "If I want to basically believe the world is a generous place—and I do want to believe this—then perhaps the world is giving us all a little better than we deserve."

And that was—perhaps surprisingly—a surprising thought.

It changed my perspective. I reconsidered certain thoughts. Some opportunities I wished for were perhaps not yet in the right time. Perhaps everything I needed for my development was available for me right now! Maybe I simply needed to keep following the path emergent. Sometimes not receiving something is in our best interest in the first place. One of the key points of this book, is that your most fundamental power lies in how you conceive of your current situation, even over the "realities" of what you are experiencing.

This concept of the generosity of the world may be unsettling, however it can motivate out of self-pity and into a state of proactive action. Instead of fixating on apparent lack, this idea can open your mind to all the great things you do have. The gift of life, and future opportunity, is a great place to start.

The next step, after considering the inherent generosity of the world, came as, "Well, if I want something more, what do I need to do to create more." This thought brought my mind to a place of proactive intention, and with it a sense of possibility and positivity. When one is freed from any aspects of a blame cycle (whether that is blame of others or yourself) is when one can find a proactive path. Trusting in the generosity of life can move one from envy to gratitude—putting responsibility and possibilities back in your court.

It is a choice. If you want to believe the world is a hard place, it is a choice. That thought can probably also be turned to advantage. For me, one of the most important aspects of a personal belief system is bringing tangible positive results—happiness for instance—to yourself and others. Use whatever system works for you.

However, I have decided I WANT to believe the world is a generous place. And then, if the world is a generous place, then that leaves me in a position of responsibility for my creation, because the world is always going to give me more than I deserve. This includes a sense of responsibility, but yet it is comforting. If, and when, we are undeserving, the world will still look out for us, more than we merit. This can be a powerful consideration. I see this as a springboard to readiness and motivation.

If you can embrace the idea the world has been generous with you, be generous with others. Find ways to forgive those in your life you can forgive. Mostly, we all do the best we can in our circumstances, sometimes we do not know any better. If you can find a sense of forgiveness, for yourself and others, this can also help you "Zen the Wave" to more freedom.

If you find someone cutting in line in front of you at the supermarket, see if you can let it go, maybe they need to be there more than you do in that time. Take the moment to think higher thoughts, your thoughts and feelings are important. Direct them to what you want.

If you must wait a couple minutes for someone to start a meeting, move your mind into the opportunity of those moments. Is there another potential or thought available for you to consider? In the stead of irritation—the opposite of Law 2—embrace your opportunity.

Irritation can be useful—it can show how deep is your want or desire for something—when you perceive you are not getting it. But as quick as you can, switch your mind to what is important! The FLOW of life, your good feelings, staying focused and using your skills, catching the potential of the moment...to "Zen the Wave." These are the important principles.

We have all been caught in unproductive thought patterns. However, the more effort we put into our thought development and the higher we progress, it becomes easier to stay in more productive patterns. Shirley Verrett, my wonderful teacher and mentor at the University of Michigan mentioned once a discovery she made. That is, as a career progresses, one seems to more often find individuals who are able to correlate to these ideas, this context here named... "Zen the Wave."

UNIVERSAL ZEN—IT WILL WORK FOR YOU

This is the point in the book where I hope to answer any doubts you might hold regarding if this system will work for you. As you begin to embrace these ideas, some individuals might agree with all these thoughts in principle, but when it comes to themselves, just feel as if they might not be worthy. One might feel somehow that they are the exception to the rule or "law."

Recently, I had an experience meeting someone and discussing the FLOW Law concepts. He stated in a theoretical way he appreciated the principles. But because of his own personal background, and because of this or that, he questioned if the system would function for him. He felt doubt in his chances for progress.

This is the point to express, nothing about your past, background or station matters in the FLOW. Certainly, there are people born with advantages of wealth or station. Some families have a history in politics, and with wealth and prestige along with it, this could assuredly give advantage for someone starting out in specific dreams.

But here is an especially important point. Your past does not dictate your life adventure from right now. Your excitement—your best path, your advancement, your unique life experience that will never be completely recreated in time—is available for you from this moment forward. Gaining that understanding will help you fully engage in these laws, and then it can be a magnificent experience.

These concepts are for absolutely everyone reading this, but remember, only if you allow it. And if you do not believe, I would say this is simply from not truly understanding the system and / or getting yourself in the way. You can address that by Law 5, "Zen the Wave." Ultimately, your success is never dependent on any external measure of success, your success is simply commitment to living your path to the fullest, and that is available to all of us at every moment, if we simply choose it.

We can never fully grasp the course of another's life, and this understanding can be a great resource to find compassion. That said, the FLOW is universal, available to everyone, right now. And in this FLOW, satisfaction, joy, and gratitude are practically guaranteed, and miraculous advancement just might be a part of the journey.

ZEN IT BIG

Having a "big ego" or unrealistic dreams can be a problem, but so can selling yourself short. Maybe your issue is you need more confidence? Maybe you need to shoot higher or think more of yourself? And your needs can sometimes shift, one moment you may need to be more realistic, and the next you may need to just think big. Sometimes, you just need to "Zen it big."

Often, we may hear someone has a "big ego", and this is seen as not a great thing, it is often seen as undesirable. And perhaps an individual with too big of an ego—or only interested in a small world view and not sensitive to the needs of others—is an issue. Or someone may think too highly of themselves or their ability, beyond the actual scope of their current situation.

However, there is the reverse of this which can play out if your conception of yourself is too limited. It can in turn vastly limit your potential. You need to find your strengths and believe into them fully. Know your worth and find projects that grow with your potential.

I find more and more, mediocre projects are less likely to work out for me than when I aim for higher goals! If you find yourself working at better, higher, or more intense levels, go with it. My work with the FLOW Laws has been going on for a long time. Sometimes now when I think something is "just good enough," my FLOW will come along and say, "There is more available to you than you think!" My FLOW will drop the mediocre to give space for the extraordinary.

If an experience, or a job, or a relationship dissolves, it can be disconcerting. However, there may be something better right around the corner. In the end you might be grateful for the change.

As mentioned, career options in my life, which I thought of as opportunities, dissolved when I had hoped them to continue. I felt emotional about it, but later realized what a blessing it was to be able to move on. Much greater opportunities were on the way and the more I could trust my FLOW, the more ease I had moving into my success.

Then when something appears you genuinely do want, go for it! If it is better than you have ever thought possible, give it a chance. Do not quickly toss your manifestation because of concerns of unworthiness, when the world makes a fantastic offer, in general, say, "Yes!" When a time has come for you, and you know it, rise to the occasion and make yourself worthy, and stay open to learn as you go.

Keep flexibility in your mind, especially towards your own benefit. Beliefs about your life are one of the most important determining factors in your existence. Why believe in limiting ideas about your potential? Why get caught in the smallest denominator of who you are? Everyone has the potential for advancement and joy in the journey, this is universal. Jump into this energy.

As more possibilities come into your life, you will need discernment. However, do not let an unduly modest opinion of yourself get in your way. Go back to FLOW Law 2, find what you love, and then "Zen the Wave."

BEYOND YOUR "SELF" AND INTO YOUR TRANSCENDENCE

"Zen the Wave," is in essence very practical, it is not mysterious, or transcendent. It is summed up in the idea, that often, all you need to do is get your limiting thoughts or personality out of the way. Then your "wave" can bring you to where you need to be. It is a common story, that individuals have been their own stumbling blocks. In "Zen the Wave" we navigate around ourselves for our greatest good.

The experience of navigating the "self" can have transformative power. As we get out of the way, or find high paths to pursue, we can develop into new and better people, with more ability and creativity. This is amazing and its own form of transcendence.

Through inspiration, you can find power to transform. For several years I have been the host of a morning radio show in Busan, South Korea. Busan is a city of several million people, the show can be accessed through the FM radio, as well as the internet and the station's app—internationally—allowing a practically limitless potential for listeners.

I have a strong belief, at any given time, someone listening to our show may need to feel uplifted and that our show will have an impact on someone's life and make it a little better. I know it is a belief, I cannot always prove it, but it helps me to "Zen the Wave."

Every time I go into the studio to record, I may not be in my best mood. However, my belief in the possibilities of what I am doing—and that there is someone out there who needs my best—helps me to transform into the best version of myself. And in radio, it must happen in that moment. In a way, it is magic.

Thus, pay attention to your impact. Pay attention to what you can bring to life and start paying attention to other people. What is it that other people need and are trying to say to you? How do others feel and what do they need? By paying attention to the world and others you can find inspiration and courage to choose your best path and "Zen the Wave."

None of us live in a vacuum, we are all connected. Your feelings and thoughts are felt by others and the world at large, probably more concretely and more fully than you can ever know. By moving more and more into your higher thoughts and motivations, you will find higher responses from the world.

There has been a lot of notice in recent time given to so called "laws of attraction," it has become something of a *Zeitgeist*. It is the idea that you get what you put out into the world. This premise does play heavily into the thesis of all the FLOW Laws and how they function. We want to feel connected, to have fun, to be a part of something that is enjoyable to us. As you "Zen the Wave" you will not only be creating more of what you want, but simultaneously be attractive *to* more of what you want.

"Zen the Wave" will give you confidence to find the best you and go with it. There are many ways you can help yourself out, by simply getting out of your own way, by streamlining your thoughts and desires... And the principles are...well, they are fun...but they do require devotion and cultivation. Get a mind like steel in the direction of your goals. Convince yourself of the universality of the FLOW, keep taking these ideas with you throughout your day. The forces and concepts we are working with are bigger than we can imagine.

Know that, as you choose to focus on the best, you will most quickly get to your best future. Relax and go with the FLOW Laws. "Zen the Wave," and your success and your enjoyment of it, will be much closer at hand.

MEDITATION
I choose to follow my higher functioning and I trust the unfolding of my path. I will do what need be done, prioritizing that which is important to me and staying focused on what I most want.

FLOW Law 6

"Honor the Waves"

It's all about the hotel room
"Tonight, I will be singing for you."
The right place at the right time
Health is wealth—as is the ability to enjoy success
Lovin' the cash
The mirror without a speck of dust
Meditation

At this very moment, you may have more "going for you" than you ever imagined. Often, we judge our lives on lack—as opposed to the fantastic blessings we already possess. Be it your health, wealth, career, relationships, family, personal traits, motivation, ambition...what "waves" do you have going for you? These are all forms of "energy." With introspection, it might surprise us how much we currently do have.

When I started work as a classical singer in New York City, it was exciting. I had found a dream, I felt passionate about it, and I had already put in the time for years and years to develop the skills I needed. Finally, the moment had come to implement all the practice and start the career, and in many ways, I was content.

As my career became more active especially throughout North America, one aspect of many engagements included a month or more spent in the far-flung cities for rehearsal periods and then performances. I would usually be housed in a comfortable hotel, and occasionally at the best hotel in town. At times this could last up to six weeks. Being on the road certainly had its ups and downs, but for the most part, it was enormously fun.

In "Honor the Waves" we take a moment to count our blessings—and realize the various skills and "energy" we possess—at this very instant in time.

IT'S ALL ABOUT THE HOTEL ROOM

While "on the road," I gained a clear example of varying attributes or energies that can be working for us, and the importance to honor them all. On site rehearsing for a concert, I was housed at a very posh resort. It was about my favorite housing for an engagement up until that point. The location was an elegant beachside resort that had been featured on popular national TV shows. It was beautiful, it was luxurious, comfortable, and included a great private beach. I felt fortunate to be there, enjoying this experience.

During off time from rehearsals and events, I was able to appreciate the hotel and frequent the beach. On one occasion, sitting out by the water, I met an elegant investment banker. She and her children had flown in from overseas to stay at this hotel. She was charming, eloquent, and I enjoyed the time to chat with her. Ultimately, I gleaned several insights from this experience.

In the course of conversation, we visited the topic of our varied backgrounds. My development in the world of the arts and her study in finance leading to her position. We were both content with our life paths, however, we each had experiences for which the other was curious.

For her, it seemed a privilege to work in the field of the arts, honing skills and creating beautiful experiences for others. Also, I could see she relished the idea of learning and developing as an artist in general—and some of the fantastic personalities and celebrities I interacted with on this career path intrigued her. For myself, I found the concept of closing deals in a high-level corporate environment grand—along with the clear sense of financial benefit that would result.

Traveling for the singing career up until that point, I had nothing but joy at my hotel stays. Spending time at an elite hotel was a blast—and a thrill when included as a career perk. However, suddenly, as I considered our relative positions, I realized had I booked a hotel myself, most likely I would have opted for a more economical hotel choice rather than this seemly extravagant hotel.

With nothing changed save perspective, I now saw my hotel stay as somehow "less valid." I had not purchased it on my own, and I suddenly felt I was "only there" because I was on a job. And that thought, for a short period, diminished my pleasure.

Thankfully, I did not maintain this thought train for long and this experience became a wonderful awakening, providing impetus to rethink my position. I had two basic realizations, the most important being the fact that I *was* there at the hotel was reason enough to be there--and to appreciate it. It did not matter what forces brought me to that moment in time on the beach. Also, a secondary idea I gleaned from this experience was an encouragement to further my financial intelligence and to go for more.

Again, nothing had changed but perspective when facing my status at the hotel. Perspective is vastly important. It is amazing how quickly our thoughts can change our experiences. If I had allowed myself into a less gracious thought process, it would not have served me. And I wish to keep luster and magic in my experience, and I want to enjoy life to the fullest.

Thus, there was no correlation, I decided, between cash on hand and how one could enjoy the sunset on that beach. This realization of "Honor the Waves" was born. Whatever collection of events brings you where you are, is valid. Whether the experience was purchased through cash or credit, or from skill from a job, we all had landed at the same beach. We all had the opportunity to enjoy the same sunrise from a beautiful hotel.

Everyone working at the hotel was also privy to these beautiful surroundings, the luxury of the place. It was a wonderful location to spend time, even if on a job. All of us together were privileged with the splendor of this natural world. With these thoughts I felt a shared experience and deeper sense of connection with my environment.

It is true there is no price tag on the most important aspects of our existence. One of our most important abilities then, is the ability to ENJOY. Our ability to find freedom in the moment itself, and not the specific means that brought us there.

Now, I am all about earning and growing financial wealth and the sense of freedom this entails. This is one very direct form of wealth (or wave) to "honor." This was the secondary idea I gleaned from this experience, and we will explore this idea a little more in a later section in this law. However, most importantly at that moment, I realized, in a slightly new way, just having more cash does not assure satisfaction of life. Finding satisfaction in life is primary, and then allow the FLOW to follow through with the details.

After the time at that resort, I did spend more effort on financial aspects of life and developed more interest in investing. Part of my study also lead me to become licensed as a real estate agent in NYC. But the main realization was to keep enjoying everything I already had. If others seem to have "more," how can it help to encourage us on our path? Your perspective is the key to the enjoyment of your experiences.

Author photo, Waldorf Astoria New York, Gala

"TONIGHT, I WILL BE SINGING FOR YOU."

A few years after the time at the resort, I sang at a momentous event at the Waldorf Astoria New York in NYC. It was my privilege to commence the event and program for the night by singing, including the National Anthem. Later in the evening, the main sensation of the day was Lady Gaga and a surprise appearance of Tony Bennett.

While at the venue early to warm up on the stage, I ran into an elegant woman in the hall. We struck up a quick and witty conversation, and it was only later that I realized this cultured—and youthful lady—was the mother of Lady Gaga!

As the evening progressed and as I finished singing my part at the gala, I received a message from the director of the affair for the evening. "Cynthia was hoping you might come and have a chat at the table." My mind blanked for a second, "Cynthia...?"

"Lady Gaga's Mom!"

"Oh, yes, of course!" Certainly, I wished to visit and chat with the family Gaga. Through that initial contact with Lady Gaga's mother at the rehearsal, and by apparently doing a decent enough rendition of the National Anthem, I had an opportunity to meet and speak with the entire family. They presented themselves as personable, open, down to earth people. Through this meeting I was also introduced to Lady Gaga by her mother.

I was told later it was unusual for Lady Gaga to open up quickly with a new person, but perhaps as she had just heard me sing, the music was its own form of introduction. For what must have been 20-30 minutes we connected on all sorts of topics, from being musicians, about the track she was on in her art at the time, my experience moving to Korea...about life in general.

Perhaps feeling at ease and connecting with her as a fellow human being and musician, *honoring my waves*, rather than being simply in awe of the pop icon, allowed her to be more at ease as well. That evening I was surfing my wave, enjoying my life and I simultaneously "Honor-ed the Waves" of whatever skill and chance allowed me to have been there. And she seemed genuinely interested in my own career path, having packed up my bags from NYC and moved to Asia, specifically South Korea. We spoke a little about South Korea in general, and I left with the impression she even liked Korean food!

As we wrapped up our conversation, she paused and looked at me in a meaningful way. "Will you be here when I sing tonight?" she asked. I told her, of course I would be. That is when I had a taste of Lady Gaga, *pop icon*. In a stylized movement, she leaned her full body to the left side, head pivoting to the right and pointing her right arm and hand directly at me declared,

"Tonight...I will be singing for you."

It was a big night.

It was out of this world. As I "Honor-ed the Waves" and kept in the joy of the moment, I took the evening at face value for what the FLOW offered.

By following the FLOW Laws, you will have more courage to take a hold of opportunities when presented. And keep hope, there are always new experiences available. We keep growing and developing, when you find yourself in a new position, it does not matter how you got there. Enjoy, and make use of the moment.

THE RIGHT PLACE AT THE RIGHT TIME

This experience with Lady Gaga is a wonderful, if extraordinary, example of being in the right place at the right time—and that this ability is one of the greatest forms of wealth. As much as we can and should value material wealth—why block it—appearing at the right place at the right time is perhaps the greatest treasure a person can have.

Your life itself, and its FLOW, is your most valuable possession on earth. The FLOW is a form of energy and wealth, and this ability should be truly honored. Being in the right place at the right time is one of the greatest gifts to have. This principle can make everything happen.

Carl Jung held great interest in and researched the idea of synchronicities. This is also related to the idea of being in the right place at the right time. He noted a story of a woman who lost her wedding ring, only later to find it when slicing a potato, inside the potato. The chances of something like this taking place are astronomically unlikely. I have had some extreme examples of synchronicity from my own life...how one played out for me was quite fascinating.

While living in New York City, my sister and I had just stepped off the subway train at a Sunset Park station in Brooklyn, NY. Sunset Park is an area in Brooklyn that has arguably the best views of Manhattan in the world, and along with that, it holds some of the many favorite Mexican restaurants in New York City. We were headed to a Mexican food gem on Brooklyn's *5th Ave.*

As we had been on the subway and as we were exiting, my sister and I conversed about this concept of time and place and ideas that would later become the FLOW Laws. Specifically, we spoke about this aspect of life, that as one moves further along into the FLOW Laws, it can be as if the world works in tandem with oneself—and might even leave clues along the way.

We were having fun with the ideas, walking and talking, and as we passed a bench on the way out of the station, I took notice of a book seated on the bench. I felt something in my *self* drawn to it, turned to my sister and said, "This book is left here for me!"

She looked at me askance, lifted her eyebrows with a hint of curiosity and said, "Ok, sure, whatever you say."

I picked up the book and flipped it open. It opened directly to a page number with personal significance, and I thought that was it. It seemed like an unusual coincidence, but what came next stopped me, and my sister, in our tracks. In the center of the page there was a blank space and within it was written these words as a quote.

> "To Cristofero,
> whose love of learning is almost as great
> as his love of beauty."[2]

I have experienced many coincidences in my life—this one was breathtaking. (Also, I should mention, my Italian cousins always have addressed me as *Cristofero*.) The chances of identifying a book on a bench, calling it out, and having that specific of a message seemed at infinitesimally small odds.

Of course, I am not a statistician, yet I felt a sense of circumstance speaking directly to me. One can interpret this type of experience as one wishes; however, for me a feeling of import was strong. And my take is if this feeling can provide positive, tangible, proactive energy—and gain result from it—why not go with it? At that moment at least, I did pick up the right book, in the right place and at the right time.

HEALTH IS WEALTH—AS IS THE ABILITY TO ENJOY SUCCESS

Relatively recently I had an opportunity to join in on a seminar featuring new technologies, future growth, future direction of society—the world of cutting-edge thought. While there, I hit it off with a successful, and still relatively young businessman. He had been living an extreme and dramatic lifestyle, and we shared with each other our stories.

A few years before, he arrived at having created companies valued into the multi-million dollars of worth. He was remarkably successful. But on the way, he did a bang-up job to exhaust his body. At one point, he told me, he felt he would have traded everything back for feeling the way he had ten years before.

Now, the happy side to this story is after that revelation, he altered his focus and begun training his mind into more positivity. He started following his own style of meditating, followed a new life protocol, and step by step he experienced a great rejuvenation. His rejuvenation was extreme, he told me he even had regeneration of ligaments that had been said to be unlikely, if not impossible, to regrow.

This inspired me. First as a reconfirmation of the possibility to recover health, and then also in the thought that health is truly a form of wealth. If you are feeling fit and well, you have the world by the tail, this is one of the greatest forms of wealth. If you feel well, even relatively well, celebrate it! And if you need to regenerate, know that great possibility exists for you, just follow the path emergent to your health.

LOVIN' THE CASH

The right mindset is one of the greatest forms of wealth. But what about the world of dollars and cents, stocks and bonds, foreign currency, and the gold and precious metal markets? Having wealth available, having liquidity, and having direct access to it is a fantastic resource, it is a form of energy. Accessible monetary wealth can also be a support to those around us.

Everyone's path to material wealth is individual. The idea that cash in the bank is a form of wealth, is obvious, but still bears brief discussion. Though most of us value "money"— and maybe even want more of it—there can be hang-ups, or misconceptions, about the "cash" that can be useful to address.

Many movements, or traditions, throughout history have taught ideas of the renunciation of material existence in order to gain greater connection to a conceptual or spiritual world. Individuals still carrying these inclinations, might have an idea that acquiring some or any personal wealth could affect their connection to spirit. Along with these ideas, or other unique personal experiences, there can be various associations in relationship to money. It is useful, at various points, to sit down and consider how you feel about the idea of money and your personal relationship to it.

What are your associations with the idea of money? Are they positive ones? Do you feel balance around the idea in your life? It is often in our best interest to let money FLOW in a sense of trust, and even fun around the idea. If for some reason you have an idea that wealth is lacking on spirit, or if you have other related conceptions, perhaps it is worth some time to consider that?

How are your ideas on money affecting you? You might find other hang-ups around money, even the idea that you are convinced you will never have enough. The world is a changing place, visit ideas that will be of benefit to you, including that you can achieve a state of financial security. Your thoughts about money are important, and it is a valuable process to reevaluate your thoughts with new ideas from the FLOW system.

Certainly, if one values monetary gain above all else, this can lead to out-of-sync behavior. This requires a balancing, being in your FLOW is a primary concept, and then let the steps to your wealth follow.

"Money" and its enjoyment within the proper context is a powerful form of energy. Financial security is a natural and worthy goal. By developing a healthy attitude towards "the cash," and following your FLOW, time should bring more secure financial positions. Honor money as a tangible stream of energy, and this also stems from developing an abundant approach to existence.

THE MIRROR WITHOUT A SPECK OF DUST

In closing Law 6, I would like to review the idea that everything stems from our minds. Our experiences start from our thoughts and our underlying beliefs, and then play out in the material world. Keeping our mind sharp and clear is a most valuable form of wealth.

To rephrase a story from Chan Buddhism,[3] there was a group of ancient philosophers who competed to prove who best understood the "Way" or the "Path." The long and short of it was a debate on the nature of "mind." The "mind" was by one senior practitioner likened to a "mirror without a speck of dust." The debate went on further with the idea there was never a "mind" in the first place... This gets deep, however, what I wish to focus on for practical use, is this image of the "mirror without a speck of dust." This is the idea of a keen, clean, and bright mind.

The longer I find myself on this planet, the more I am convinced that having a sharp mind is one of the greatest assets you can have—and is a form of wealth. It runs with the idea that human capital is the greatest form of capital. And even though keeping your mind sharp is one of the greatest forms of wealth—it can be kept up at an exceptionally low cost. The main price is your motivation to do so.

Do you follow practices that you feel can keep your mind sharp? Reading this book is an example. There are so many ways and angles to address this issue, including: physical activities, projects of learning, meditations, and even card games or games in general.

In ancient Asia the warriors, the nobility—even just cool old people—they would all practice calligraphy to keep the mind sharp, along with other various art forms. Studying the FLOW Laws is a great way to sharpen your mind. There are innumerable ways to work on the focus of our minds, even a walk in the park using skills of observation can be helpful. What a wonderful form of energy this is, and available to us at any moment! Keep finding practices or daily exercises with the focus of keeping your mind sharp!

Keeping the mind sharp throughout our lives—in our youth and as we age—is another of our greatest treasures. In closing, money is wealth, health is wealth, being in the right place is wealth, friends and family are wealth, and just being alive on this planet is an incredible form of wealth. Let's honor them all!

MEDITATION

I value the power of all my assets; of my skills, in finding the right timing, of cash on hand, and in keeping my mind sharp. I value that wealth is flowing from my connection to existence, which is abundant, and through which I find the power and connections to make all things happen.

FLOW Law 7

"Surf the Wave"

Getting back on the wave
Practicalities and "Surf the Wave"
The pearl of great price
The idea of sacrifice
Motivation to keep going—can you love it enough
Meditation

Even if all cylinders are firing, and one is fully on track, following your FLOW and the FLOW Laws can take some focus. And Life can still present its challenges and tests. In my prior described trip to India, everything moved like clockwork and then at the last minute, it was as if a test appeared for me.

Do you really want to finish a project? Are you willing to go the extra mile? Can you figure your way around your interactions with others with more skill, more grace, more fun? Will your creativity come in for you? Be kind to yourself and others, let yourself and others off the hook and get up and go, again and again, even if you feel you *wiped out*. And as you keep refining these various steps, the process will get easier. One analogy that comes to mind, in life in general as well as in specific projects, is that of the wood carver.

In the beginning the carver has the block of wood, and an idea. As the carver starts the project, at the outset, there is more effort to get through the layers of wood. As the project, or life in general, continues, more of the base levels of effort is completed and work can focus on detail. Wood has already been shed, and it becomes time for sanding or refining the piece. The more we understand the processes, all the various levels will be easier—but sometimes we can still use encouragement.

Keep up with your dreams, day by day! It takes commitment and follow-through to make a major impact. And sometimes, it feels Life has a built-in mechanism to make sure we get the lesson. Let's be worthy to pass the test and move on to the next level with flying colors.

This is the domain of FLOW Law 7.

GETTING BACK ON THE WAVE

If the temple visit described at the beginning of the book had been completely smooth, I would have had an easier day, but a less exciting journey. And the story for this book would have been truncated, or not as interesting. In the end everything worked out, and it often does, when you are working in tandem with your FLOW.

These FLOW Laws are meant to be incorporated as a daily practice. It is an on-going process, and it is continuous. As you keep working with the process, it can feel more and more that you are in your groove or riding your wave, and everything becomes easier. However, the point is that life is a work in process, and this is something to remember.

Every day you keep implementing these laws, and though you may never be able to go completely on autopilot (and honestly, who would want to) you will find that as you keep refining your skills, the process of staying on track will become easier and easier. Your life will FLOW into more desirable experiences and generally more of what you want. You will find joy in living skillfully.

An early memory I have of getting back up and going, even if you "wipe out," comes from childhood. It relates to an older neighbor who became a good friend of our family. He originally hailed from a little village at the top of a mountain in Northern Italy. He was an agreeable and charming man, had great stories, and we would sometimes take bike rides together.

One day we were riding down a bike path, I was first to arrive at a dip where a pool of water had covered our way. The bike tires slid from under me and I had a spectacular slide all along the path. My bike and I finally came to stop in a deep puddle. My clothes were soaking wet. I was shaken, but wanting to keep my "game face," I pulled myself up directly, squeezed myself off, and got back on the bike.

I noticed our neighbor watching me quietly and pondering for a minute. I sat on the bike soaked, paused, and looked at him. And I waited for his reaction. He mused a moment more and then said, "Now that's what I like. You keep getting up, again and again, and you never stop trying."

Again, it is a memory I will never forget. And I will never know what he was thinking at that moment. Maybe all the times in his life when he needed to pick himself up and start over. Maybe he saw some spark of determination in me and he wanted to fan that flame. Sometimes if we are lucky enough to have learning experiences as children, they can make an impact, and we can remember them our whole lives.

PRACTICALITIES AND "SURF THE WAVE"

As your life starts moving—picking up speed and momentum—and moving with bigger waves as it were, that is a chance for more learning. When you start taking action, that is when you are able to test yourself. Do not be surprised if you discover new aspects of yourself, or even feel overwhelmed.

You do not learn what you are made of without a little pressure. As you get life moving in the directions of your dreams, you start to understand more your strengths, as well as your areas for improvement.

Also, any underlying concerns will come to the forefront as you face more numerous and higher-level responsibilities. This is normal, so you need not question yourself if you notice insecurities. And as these new concerns or aspects of yourself come to the surface, you need not feel you are lacking. It is normal to have concern and questions, keep your wits about you and keep employing what you have learned.

As the stakes get higher, it is a normal response to face even your unspoken fears. As you go, take stock of how you are doing, and consider that it is often a good thing to start out on smaller scale projects or levels to learn and gain confidence. This is a point to repeat and to catch onto, life can happen very fast, but there are still skills one often needs to develop—and I also do not usually believe in jumping steps.

This was mentioned before, move through steps quickly, but try not skipping them entirely...and you can move through steps incredibly fast! As you gain confidence in smaller projects and have more success to your name, you will have more confidence to take on larger issues. If you want to develop an extraordinary life, you may be called on to gain skills, personal and otherwise, (such as in reading this book), and then put in the effort to manage it.

As you make use of the FLOW system, you will be continuing to hone your ability. You will be more able to "on point" switch into a state of resourcefulness. In the story at the temple, I managed to continue to my goal by constantly catching into the new and next thought. It also involved utter positivity that the goal was ultimately possible, and that the next step of the path would appear.

As you move more distances on your wave, and are feeling stronger, it can be time to take on bigger challenges. And again, you might face new levels of uncertainty. But the more you understand yourself and the general processes, you will be more able to tackle your greater desires. Pay attention to your thoughts, your actions and keeping your center. Remember, with new heights, it is normal to feel your unconscious concerns and personal weakness come to the surface.

And as you realize this is a normal part of the process, you will be more able to handle yourself and your circumstances. By staying in touch with the FLOW, and going step by step, you will have the best chances for success.

Sometimes when individuals come to self-help movements, or ideas of "manifestation" there can be a misconception of the concept of effort. We want to have a great life without undue effort, but would we want a life with absolutely no uncertainty or effort?

Part of the *fun* of life and the creative process, is the excitement of testing yourself and seeing things unfold. There is a magic not only in having life unfold without effort, but also by harnessing the power of practicality—and as mentioned, ease is relative. Just because your thoughts line up well, does not indicate your projects will be short on action. Look for inspired, uplifting, and concise action, and then see where life takes you. Maybe one person can just win the lotto, and that takes care of all financial goals. But often, you will need to pick up the phone when it rings...

Promo-photo for author as co-owner / sommelier: Share D Table restaurant, Seoul, South Korea

I learned some lessons about "Surf the Wave" from my experience as a restauranteur. One day the thought, "Let's open a star-studded critically acclaimed restaurant in Seoul, South Korea!" and then seeing the grand opening of our restaurant *Share D Table* in Sung Su Dong, Seoul with my partners—within six months—was an intense and spectacular ride. And it included passionate effort on the part of many individuals.

Yet, what excitement—deadlines looming—we grasped onto this idea for an innovative, international style, market restaurant—along with coffee and open-view cake shop with a hip and sophisticated onsite bar—in the month of October! We found a location in Seoul, designed, implemented, constructed, and opened it by the first of March.

There was a lot of intensity—and some anxiety—and this is fully normal. The more I live, the more I can embrace short periods of intensity—that might even include some anxiety—as periods of intense energy. I can embrace this feeling and register the energy as zest or excitement for life. Excitement indicates something is on its way. It might mean just lean back, sink-in and enjoy the ride, or take things a little slower for a bit...or it could be a possible sign to reangle the course. It is normal for actions to have reactions—opening a restaurant in record time—it is normal to face some intense moments! It is all in how you work with it, and that is comforting to remember.

To be in your FLOW is not to say that you will never or should never feel anxious again. If you feel anxious, that can be a great thing, too. Maybe your mind is trying to remind you of something you are forgetting. Be open for the revelation, ask yourself, "Why am I anxious, is there a valid reason for this anxiety?"

Find out if you need to investigate a new direction or look out for an unforeseen ramification. And then get back as quick as you can to enjoying the experience of the new marble countertop, for instance—it was probably a valid choice! If something goes off track, fix what you can, but then also look at the sunset for a moment and enjoy it. There is a spectrum in life, between lack of energy on one side and over-anxious on the other. It is a balance we keep working with, and some shifting in the spectrum is normal according to circumstances.

Get into the good feelings and let this carry you to FLOW. Be honest and direct, finding equanimity with what comes, because you know you are doing your best. Be easy with yourself and forgiving of others, forgiveness will help you into your FLOW and stabilize your path, as well as lighten your load. Keep making use of the FLOW Laws year by year and over time you could see vast changes in your outward life, and as well as developing inward stability.

THE PEARL OF GREAT PRICE

In university music school, the professor we study with for our primary major is an important part of our experience and music curriculum. Often students will apply to a university so that they can study with a specific individual. After my first year of undergraduate, my fantastic piano professor moved on with his career and FLOW, and I was left with what to do next.

Another pianist, Professor Yong Hi Moon, was on faculty at our university. She is a top name in the world of music and piano, an international performer and artist, and I hoped to study with her. I was excited about the prospect but to bolster my confidence—and get some added impartial insight—I did something I would not always recommend—I went in search of a fortune cookie.

Now, certainly, I will not honestly recommend you going to a fortune cookie for advice. At that moment, however, the idea struck me, and it seemed "the right thing to do." It felt as if I was following my FLOW to do it...and as I opened my cookie, I got a shock. *"In this time of loss, you will find a pearl of great price."*

I was convinced, Professor Moon must be the "pearl of great price."

The next day, I went directly to Professor Moon's studio. I approached her about taking lessons for the next term and I was thrilled with her response. "Of course, Christopher, I will accept you in my studio. You are very talented."

I kept this story about the fortune cookie from Professor Moon until years and years later. But there is one more interesting turn to the anecdote, after my first semester working with her, I gave a piano recital. She came backstage to greet me and wish me well before the concert and was wearing a necklace from which hung one shining, silvery pearl.

Keep following the FLOW of your path. Waves change directions, but if you follow your impulses and keep going, the waves will find a way to turn out for you.

THE IDEA OF SACRIFICE

What about the idea of loss or perceived loss and can we at times tie this into the idea of sacrifice? I believe the world is a magical and mysterious place. I believe there are rules functioning beyond my grasp, but which I can at times intimate and work with using such ideas as the FLOW Laws. Through this mindset, I approach various aspects of life that at first glance may not be easily comprehended.

If we put effort into a project, and it does not turn out, it is easy to feel disappointment. I take the stance that the good energy I put into life, will come back. Period. If not in a direct result now, at some point to come. The good results will come, though possibly in a different way, or time of reckoning, than first anticipated.

One has a much better chance of success by taking momentary setbacks in stride and moving forward. Of course, if there are enough setbacks, this can indicate perhaps the timing is not right or a sign to investigate other directions. There is also an idea of exchange of energy, which can include giving something up to get something more. Either in concrete terms, or in our own thought processes. It could even relate to a concept of sacrifice.

This book came to me as a well-formed idea and I was vastly excited, even surprised by it. I called a friend to share this experience immediately, it was as if I was transported to a different world. In this absorbed state I boarded the subway coming home with a *Chuseok* (Korean Thanksgiving) gift in hand, a seaweed box set. I was looking forward to this gift and was satisfied with it. Upon reaching home, however, I looked at my hand. "Where did it go?" The box set was not in my hand. "Did I put it down while on the phone, on the subway?"

I went back to the station and an attendant offered to look for the set with me. But it was nowhere to be found. Upon returning home again, I started noticing definite feelings of disappointment and loss. Then I stopped myself. I had just received this idea of a great book. It came from out of the blue and I had been elated. This revelation showed a way to reach a personal message to the world and touch possibly countless lives—and I was letting go of positive energy because of a gift box set.

It is important to come back as quickly as we can to a place of perspective and high function. Maybe that box gift set left on the train went to someone who could enjoy it more than I could. Further, perhaps even this gift could be considered an offering to life for the bigger gift of inspiration. Life gave me a book, and then I placed down a box set as a thank you. Why not? Considering the circumstances, and these ideas, I could let myself off the hook on this. I hope it can help you too.

Interesting to note, around a year after this experience, I sent my book to be registered for its copyright. It can take some time and it was a few months before I got the news the copyright was accepted.

That day after I received my copyright registration, I went to the radio studio to record my show. My producer pulled me aside as I was leaving and said, "So sorry, I have been forgetting to give you something for a few weeks." He came back in a few moments with a seaweed box set he had forgotten to give me over that year's Thanksgiving.

MOTIVATION TO KEEP GOING—CAN YOU LOVE IT ENOUGH

The final element to "Surf the Wave" is that you must simply get your heart into that which you are doing and keep it there. We are willing to go further when we have our heart into something. This relates to another mystery of life, that if you are performing a gesture you see helping others, it can also bring more energy back to you. Especially in a challenging time, I try to bring kindness to people around me.

And here is a simple method to check your motivations. Just ask yourself—are you acting out of love or fear?

One of my top-ranking orchestral engagements was with the National Arts Centre Orchestra of Ottawa. And it was a great time. All details of my stay were well-planned and well-executed by the company, starting from the limousine service that picked me up at the airport.

The driver was pleasant, talkative, and kept me entertained with stories and conversation. And he told me I was one of the more personable international artists he had driven. That was a great start to the engagement.

For the performance, I was one of the four soloists to sing in the finale of the Beethoven Ninth Symphony. The other soloists were excellent, and it was an honor that the music director for the symphony at that time would be conducting, Maestro Pinchas Zukerman.

Music rehearsals with piano, and the first musical run through with the orchestra all went well. We also had amicable chances to sit and chat together, and our maestro shared humorous and witty anecdotes of his long and illustrious career.

One issue however, I found myself developing a small cold. I managed it well, and these things can happen when one is traveling and flying around. It was not a large issue, I was in good condition in general, but the thought came to me, "Will I be ok at the performance?"

If you are not familiar with Beethoven's Ninth Symphony, the Bass or Baritone soloist commences the vocal singing in the finale. The Orchestra has been playing all symphony long and then the Bass steps up, and out of the blue, sings, *Oh, Freude!* (Joy!)

Then the work opens into some of the most marvelous poetry from the German literary tradition, the "Ode to Joy" of Schiller. This symphony is one the great works of Western culture, and not the time to feel a seasonal shift. However, through this situation I found some great thoughts that brought me to a higher level of function.

I sat alone in my hotel room and said to myself, "OK, you have a choice. Do you love this more, or do you fear it? It's a simple choice really, love it, go with it, or fear it and give up!"

I chose that by far, I loved it, despite any doubts or uncertainties, and that thought gave me energy. It reminded the point there are always uncertainties—and singing would bring so much joy for me and others. When you are in a position facing uncertainty or concern, ask yourself a question. "Can I love it more?"

By choosing to love it more, I felt confidence to step out on stage and sing in front of thousands of audience members. As I went out onto the stage, as usual, I did feel some nerves, facing fear or emotions is a part of the wave. But this time, I had something else come to the forefront demanding my attention as we walked out to commence our part.

As I progressed onto the stage and looked out into the audience, in one of the front rows, sitting content and resplendent, was a Golden Retriever. At that first glance from the stage, this canine apparition was an exact replica of the family dog we had while growing up. I am not sure if I had ever before noticed a dog in the audience in this kind of concert, it must have been a service animal to be there. And this dog's presence gave me a kind of universal assurance that everything was going to be fine, and the confidence that to "love it more" had truly been the way to go.

The FLOW Laws are not a one-day procedure. The FLOW Laws are a manual to continually employ into your future. They are cumulative. They are fun. And they require adherence, and even some focus, but it will be worth it.

Even if you are doing everything right, the waves can get big, and you can feel overawed. Success is in how you manage your situation, and how you get up and keep going. It is not defined by never making a mistake or having life work out differently than you expected. Remember, the more you "Surf the Wave," the easier it will become to keep on "Surfing the Wave."

MEDITATION

I am in a process—and "refining" is a part of the game. It is inspiring to see steps develop and I look forward to implementing them. I am compassionate with myself and others, and I trust that by sticking with the FLOW Laws, I am closer to my dreams.

PART III

Conclusion

In the FLOW Freedom Laws of the World ™, and in the stories and anecdotes which illustrated them, you have found a template which can help anyone. And if you have been seeking direction, have discovered this writing, and apply these concepts seriously to your life—you can look forward to dramatic results. Of course, results are individual and vary—changes you make are up to you and your FLOW! However, one beauty of these results is that the biggest change can happen right now—and that is in a momentary upgrading of your life vision, and thus your immediate experience. This is one of the most important changes we can ever make.

Arrange your direction and FLOW

If you have taken the time to go through these principles in this book and start to let them filter into your mind and thinking, a giant "Congratulations!" to you. You have made a big step forward in your FLOW journey.

The FLOW Laws are concise and easy to memorize. As you move through daily life, keep reminding yourself of them, incorporating the laws as need be….and see the results.

Though we have touched on relationships and other issues, such as health and financial security, the main point of the book—and the laws themselves—is how to organize your philosophic direction. Of course, as the book points out, pay attention to others, and all various specifics of life that are pertinent. In the end, only you will know and can govern your specific FLOW. Everyone has different goals and needs to pursue.

The FLOW Laws are encompassing enough to serve as guide, whatever your goals may be, in how to act and feel your best—so that the specific aspects of life will fall in line for you. By following the FLOW Laws, by filling your life with joy, it is going to spill over to those around you. You will be able to become a person who is at peace with himself / herself, and thus more available to others. And when others see your positive interactions through the FLOW Laws, and how this improves your life, they too will gain. Through your example, others will gain skills and mindsets that are more valuable than any physical possession you can ever give. Perhaps most importantly, through the course of this integration, you will discover the ability to upgrade yourself into your highest capacities, into levels of peak performance.

Let your life FLOW around new goals

There is an old philosophy and idea, you are as you think. This plays out in experience, on a variety of levels. If you think deeply, for instance, that you are smart and able—this can inspire you to take smart and able action. These thoughts might motivate you to get the training you need. This could in turn help you land a good job, if that is your mindset and goal, as an example. Or your thoughts can help you do, just whatever it is you want to do! So, in a way, how you are thinking, is fully impacting your life.

Therefore, as discussed, replace previous, less interesting thoughts, with inspiring and new uplifting thoughts. This alone can change your life and experience of it. And just as a person's flow of thought has power over his / her life, to a lesser extent but still important to mention, the thoughts of others around a person also influence that individual. One consideration in starting the FLOW Law system is that those around you may not yet be expecting the new you...

Family and friends

We tend to think in relatively similar ways to those around us—and along with this—in a very real way, our friends and family are a part of our lives. However well meaning, others may also be attached to older "models" of you, or be functioning along with your earlier, less proactive or even less "evolved" thinking patterns.

If these FLOW Laws have been inspiring to you, you might feel inclined to share them, to have the people around you take part in them. It is natural and a great impulse, and if others seem on board, then by all means share, let others know about this book. But address it gingerly, share new ideas and your dreams or goals only with individuals with whom it feels *fun* to share.

Remember, we all tend towards attachment to our own thought streams. If others do not gravitate to or are not ready for the materials presented here—or even are simply not actively interested—it's OK to just follow the ideas on your own! Others may also not be in positive mindsets to encourage you on your life's goals, and that is also, OK. Let others have their own time.

Sometimes the most profound way to lead is by example. Most important, is what changes we make, sometimes quietly, in our day-to-day lives. Following the FLOW Laws yourself, and watching them play out around you, will more than likely be your greatest impact.

Get the skills as easily as you can

As you continue unlocking your dreams, you may find a need for further education or to gain new skills to achieve your goals. Following up with more training through the FLOW Freedom Laws of the World ™ and the 5 Modalities ™ is one option. You might also consider various additional training, including seminars, online or other traditional / university education options.

Having a university education is definitely a great step for many, also as a great way to build connections. However, there are many ways to gain skills for success, and I would recommend never to let a lack of education stop you from pursuing your dreams. Sure, if you want to be a practicing medical doctor, you will need to go to school for it. However, there are numerous ways to help people achieve health that can be pursued without a decade long degree program. Again, it is a matter of tapping into your creativity and looking at the core of what you want to do.

Of course, skills are important, but in some sense, it does not matter how you get them. You do not need an MBA to start a business. however, you will need ideas, training, and study—as well as understanding of principles and concepts, and how to secure needed capital. There are many ways to learn and grow, and you can always find partners with specific skills you are lacking. Focus on the end result you want, and do not get caught up on the way. And if you are to invest resources in education, know why you are doing it, and find the most expedient way to get what you need.

In developing as a classical musician, I did spend years in university training through to a doctorate degree in the field. Classical music is a complicated art form that takes time to master, and I grew immensely during my university training. Also, my advanced degrees have proved useful to me, especially regarding teaching at universities. And for various reasons, including academic grants and scholarships I secured, it made sense for my career path to stay at a university for further training.

And though the university time provided excellent training, and some extraordinary professors, some of my most important teachers and mentors took place after I finished schooling and moved to New York City. Also, when I did move to NYC after finishing my formal university training, with a doctoral degree—but now already around 30 years of age—I had an eye opener. Having a doctorate did little to get one into the entertainment industry. (We opera singers sometimes forget that opera is not a *religion*, but a niche part of the entertainment industry).

Thus, in NYC, I was required to start again from scratch. I had to go to auditions—i.e. job interviews—where my degree meant little and I needed to prove myself by skill alone. Luckily, my skills proved sufficient and the career progressed quickly, but I realized some of the drawbacks to my path in higher education.

Had I quit university earlier and applied for what basically corresponds to internship training at professional opera companies, I might have progressed professionally quicker. Having professional skills and connections earlier, could have led more directly to quicker professional success.

Therefore, in today's society, I recommend approaching creatively the field of education by finding exactly the skills you need and the quickest way to obtain them. This at times could be enrolling in a traditional degree program, but as mentioned now there are so many other avenues for education, including online certification programs, mentorship programs, seminars, you name it. And there is something to say about jumping in right where you are and learning as you go.

Your FLOW team and the idea of mentorship

It is important for almost all of us to find a support group and pay attention to them, this includes your family, your friends, and partners. Follow your own life direction to create the relationships that are right for you and serve various functions for your life. At times being alone to introspect can be great, but in general we are social creatures and having a supportive network of friends and family can be tantamount to success.

As you become more open and positive you will find better relationships developing, along with more opportunities than you could ever hope to fill. If you want to meet people, get yourself excited about life, and make yourself into someone people want to meet. Then, put yourself out where others can also find you. Find those who are open with you and on board, individuals who are amplifying your positive drive. No one is perfect, but as you can, find those who want to follow the FLOW and move in that greater current with you.

Trust that by being in the *current* you will find your team. If others are surfing their boards elsewhere, that is also ok. Know you will have as much love and friendship and support as you need. This trust is paramount, it is a trust in all that is and your place in it.

Having a guidebook such as this one is a remarkable advantage. Then having a support group, and / or personal mentors can also be especially important. Perhaps you will find friends, or a group, in which you can support each other in a mutual way to learn and grow together, staying motivated and on track. I have described some of my mentors in this book, and the positive impact working with those who have spent long effort mastering their own FLOW in their specific fields and in general.

Also, as mentioned, along with the FLOW Freedom Laws of the World ™ book, I have been currently offering seminars, programs, and there is the additional system of learning, the 5 Modalities ™. Through this program, and the related training and community, I am looking to create methods of continued support for those interested in developing themselves and their skills in the ideas of FLOW mastery.

Belizean coastline

Keep following the dream

There are a couple of ways to follow your dreams... those *dreams* or goals you have in your daily or conscious existence... And then there are those dreams you experience sleeping.

Now, personally, I am not that often receiving cues from my sleeping state. But occasionally I have come to ideas while sleeping, and that has helped me in making decisions and in how to follow my FLOW. Living in Asia, many here seriously consider images and experiences in dreams. This is, of course, the case around the world and in many cultures—but I find this especially in traditionally-minded aspects of culture in the East. If various symbols or images come up in dreams, particularly around important times, many individuals will pay attention to this and look for vital messages.

If you find yourself in a conundrum about actions to take, you can keep a watch on your dreams. Maybe the dream state will give you a clue to timing your daily-life *dreams*. You can ask others for advice about the meaning of your dreams, but in the end, it will be you alone to make the final call on what you are discovering in the sleeping state.

The first time I traveled to Belize, I took a big green backpack and I started off around the country. I had a trip planned that was to take me from North to South. Lodgings were booked and a travel itinerary was set. However, as the trip progressed, I found aspects that called my attention. I felt *called* to a more central / northern area around the capital. It was there I later made some wonderful friends, including on a farm named after a prominent geographical feature. With these friends I would discover many wonders of Belize, including the sweetness of Mangoes, still warm from the sun, as plucked from the tree.

Thus, on that specific tour, I started to question if I should take the journey to the south... The area I was staying in was exceptionally beautiful, near the main highway leading from the capital to the ocean towards the south east. The highway is named the "Hummingbird," after the way it weaves and turns through the mountains, like the flight of the hummingbird. It is one of the most picturesque drives in Central America.

I was in a bit of a quandary of where to go, as I did not wish to change all my plans. Beginning travels further south, I slept one night, and dreamt of the most beautiful flowering tree. It had giant blossoms of iridescent color and many butterflies and hummingbirds were making their way around the tree. As if the name of the highway did not correspond enough, I had even seen hummingbirds in that area.

Once I awoke in the morning from the dream, I knew my path had found a new destination. I cancelled the other appointments and made new plans to head back north to the *Hummingbird*. And I was glad I did. This was perhaps the clearest story of when a dream solidified my mind on a direction. As you pay attention to your dreams when awake, you just might get clues from your sleeping ones as well.

Watch and enjoy the FLOW

As I have mentioned, when you start out on this FLOW journey, it can feel like more effort to get your FLOW going. It can be comparable to navigating a canoe into the current of a river, you might need to put some effort in getting the direction of your trajectory in line, but once you do, you can start to watch the current pick up and take you along.

To conclude, a final fascinating example demonstrates how the FLOW of life can bring us our wishes. It can bring about circumstances to manifest dreams, even when we have forgotten them—and in ways that we might never had fathomed as possible.

When I was a child, I watched the movie "Annie," main character played by actress Aileen Quinn. We were around the same age when I saw the film, and I remember seeing this movie and having the thought I wanted to meet her. It was a pure desire of childish delight and I did not give it much thought. I never considered it truly a possibility, and I never attempted to follow up on it. This idea quickly faded, but it was nonetheless a very genuine wish when it took place, and perhaps some part of me never completely forgot that idea to meet her.

Fast forwarding my life a little over 20 years into the future, after I moved to New York City, a stage director friend asked me for a favor. She said there was a new play with which she was experimenting and asked if I would stop by to assist in a read-through. She expressed, it would be an enjoyable night, she would later invite me to dinner as a thank-you, however, it was going to be an exceptional group of talented individuals; and she wished me to be there.

The details of the event were a little mysterious, but I respected this director's thoughts and showed up for the reading. As I arrived, I discovered the actors reading that night had high levels of expertise—on the live theatrical stage, in Musical Theater, as well as in film. Walking up to the central table we were to sit around for the reading, I noticed there was one young lady already perusing the script.

With distinctive reddish hair, she had arranged herself angled from the edge of the table. Focusing on the page, she was absent-mindedly kicking one leg up and down that was crossed over the other. I wondered how that form seemed so familiar, and it hazily dawned on me, this corresponded to iconic body language from the role of "Annie" in the aforementioned feature film.

And sure enough, I walked over and was introduced to Aileen Quinn. This childhood dream, upon which I never followed up, by the mystery of happenstance, was able to come to pass. And a little stranger still, when we were introduced, it was almost as if we recognized each other. We wondered together out loud could have we met somewhere previously—at a performance, at a studio? I mused later if my wish to meet her had crossed time... Or perhaps I knew all along that it would happen—and maybe in a subtle way she felt that, too.

The more one's life has coincidences line up, the more one might feel a sense of awe in the process of living. Even as if there are forces that help coincidence along the way. And one might wonder, "Why do I not trust into my life, wellbeing, and future even more?!"

The world is a mysterious place. I believe when our minds align in more efficient ways, when we incorporate the FLOW Laws, we start having more such positive experiences. We hook into potential that is all around us. We can even feel this effect without needing to line up every detail. Arriving at a place of trust, coupled with inspired action, seems to allow experience to come in its own time.

We can actively remind ourselves to heighten our awareness to the good things around us all the time. As discussed, there is the possibility that by upgrading our performance level, we are simply able to utilize opportunities which are already there. However, it can feel magical. This happens as we create the atmosphere for our best potential to step forward.

The more skillfully you surf the FLOW, the more "good days" can come. As when I spent time with the Mayan shamans in Guatemala, every morning one of the shamans would say, "It is (X) day of the Mayan calendar, and it is a good day." And the next day, "Today is the day of (X) and it is a good day" ...and so on...

Chosŏn-era pagoda (eight-sided tower), Seoul, South Korea

Unlocking an 8th Law

As implied—and stated explicitly—throughout this text, these laws are all interrelated. You can think of this idea as the unlisted Law 8, that all the laws are in essence one set.

Being in your FLOW or to "Catch the Wave" (FLOW Law 1) can give you a philosophy of life and free you up from searching for your meaning. This state can spring you into good feelings or "Love the Wave" (FLOW Law 2). This will inspire you with energy and enthusiasm to hone your direction and direct your life in "List the Wave" (FLOW Law 3). This will in turn bring you to a position in which you are more able to take advantage of the window of time "Time the Wave" (FLOW Law 4). And as you do this while getting out of your own way "Zen the Wave" (Law 5) along with valuing all of your skills and assets, all forms of energy "Honor the Waves" (Law 6), you will be set to commit to the unfolding process in each and every day in "Surf the Wave" (Law 7).

This is the final concept, that by following any of the laws separately, they will assist you. However, when you bring them all together—there is an interrelation of the system where all laws are functioning as one. This is the state of your final completion of the FLOW System. In this eighth Law of completion, the seven Laws find a balance and the circle of the FLOW Laws is complete.

With your new understanding from these laws, you should feel empowered for life in a way that perhaps you never did before. Like a wheel, keep spinning these laws, and let that law which most pertains to your current situation guide you. These laws are FLOW Freedom Laws of the *World* ™. By reiterating this, I wish to state that no matter where in the world you find yourself, these laws can assist you. Congratulations for your investigation into the freedom giving principles. Follow your FLOW, Freedom Laws of the World ™.

MEDITATION

In this moment, I integrate the complete FLOW Laws. In this moment, the full potential of my being is present and my meaning with it. I can deeply enjoy this reality and by following the Way made apparent, in the right time, with the right spirit, and with perseverance, my dreams can and will be made manifest.

Endnotes

1. ^ *Deus ex machina*, is a literary device beginning in ancient Greek theater where a god would appear in a drama, often to solve or resolve a seemingly impossible situation.
2. ^ Dunant, Sarah, *The Birth of Venus: A Novel*, Random House Trade Paperbacks, USA: 2004, p. 175.
3. ^ *Chan* Buddhism is the Chinese variant of a school of Buddhism which would appear as *Sŏn* Buddhism in Korea and *Zen* in Japan.

Author

Photo credit: Won Seok Chang

Dr. Christopher Temporelli, DMA, is the founder / CEO of Apollo Naturopathics, LLC (www.apollonatur.com). He is an author, radio host, international classical singer, and musician. He has served as professor at numerous South Korean Universities and his credits include the world's most prestigious venues, including: *Carnegie Hall* in New York City, the *Kennedy Center* in Washington D.C., and the *Seoul Arts Center*, in Seoul, South Korea. He is a traveler, business entrepreneur, martial artist, master coach and the creator of the FLOW Freedom Laws of the World ™ and the 5 Modalities ™ systems of personal development.

www.ingramcontent.com/pod-product-compliance
Lightning Source LLC
Chambersburg PA
CBHW072158200426
43209CB00074B/1940/J